THE MANY FACES OF DEPRESSION

HOW TO BE HAPPY

God's Gift of Peace and Joy

Helen Glowacki

Forward by Daniel Patrick Landolfi

Photo selection by Colette van Loggerenberg

Novels by Helen Gumienny Glowacki

When God Broke Grandma's Heart
When God Took Grandma Home
When Grandma Chased the Spirits
The Granddaughter and the Monkey Swing
Grandma's Little Book of Poetry: The Story of God's Plan of Salvation
Abiding Faith, Hidden Treasure
And Then They Asked God

Why God Why Series by Helen Glowacki

To What Purpose?
Why God Why?
Why Trust Scripture?
What Should I Know About Life after Death And The Coming Tribulation?
What Does God Want Me To Do RIGHT NOW?
Do The Little Sins *Really* Count?

Other non-fiction Books by Helen Glowacki

Politically Incorrect: The Get Some Gumption Bible Study When Enough is Enough
The Many Faces of Depression: How to be Happy
What No One Is Telling You about Addictions

****

Authors Website: www.Helenglowacki.com

Face book: http://www.facebook.com/pages/The-Grandmother-Series/155300907853909?ref=ts

THE MANY FACES OF DEPRESSION

HOW TO BE HAPPY

God's Gift of Peace and Joy

Helen Glowacki

Forward by Daniel Patrick Landolfi

Photo selection by Colette van Loggerenberg

Library of Congress Control Number:
ISBN Hardcover
Softcover ISBN 978-1-4507-9077-2
EBook ISBN

This book was printed in the United States of America

The King James Version (KJV) of the Bible, which is public domain in the United States of America, is used for all scriptural references throughout this book. The application of which is based upon the opinion, research and religious belief of the author.

Cover by Darren Robinson, dr design & associates

Photography by Peter Herring, Anthony Hicks, Martin Lansberg, Janet Lourens, Leon Meyer, Roland Edgar Adams, Matt Burniston, Dave Campbell and Colette van Loggerenberg. Photo selection, edit and overlay by Colette van Loggerenberg, SA

To order additional copies of this book visit
www.Helenglowacki.com
For more information email Helen@helenglowacki.com

MISSION STATEMENT

TO SERVE

GOD

WITH ALL OUR

STRENGTH

AND

ALL OUR HEART

Helen Glowacki, Daniel Patrick Landolfi

ACKNOWLEDGEMENTS

Special thanks to Danny Landolfi for allowing me to use a portion of His book titled *Attitude to Conquer* for the forward of this book and for the help he provides in the publication of my books.

Thanks to Colette van Loggerenberg of Pietermaritzburg, South Africa, who selected, edited, and added verse overlays to the photographs used in this book. Thanks to Matthew Burniston, Ambrose Damon, Colette van Loggerenberg, and Raphael Wyngaart for their help in promoting my books in England and South Africa and for distributing them to those who hunger to learn the word of God. Thanks to Darren Robinson for his meticulous work on the covers.

Thanks to all the wonderful people behind the scenes who help donate my books to substance abuse and cancer centers, mission schools, and prisons around the world.

I send special love and thanks to my husband Wally who provides so much support to my work and makes my computer behave, and to my children and grandchildren for the constancy of their love and encouragement

Thanks to Rev. Kevin Speranza for locating and developing additional venues for the distribution of my books and for his loving advice, support and encouragement. Thanks to Richard Levinson for providing the first opportunity through which I could develop this work. And special thanks to my brothers and sisters and ministers in faith who give so freely of their love and prayers, and to my Face book friends who pray for me and who also support this ministry.

But most of all, my heartfelt, humble thanks to our Heavenly Father for His inspiration, guiding hand, protection, and never-ending love. May this work bring joy to His heart and help find that last soul!

NOTE TO THE READER

Depression can be a serious condition requiring the help of a medical professional. It may also require medication and ongoing medical supervision. This book and the advice therein are not meant to be a substitute for professional help. If the symptoms of depression continue, the reader is advised to seek professional help immediately.

The non-fiction books by Helen Glowacki represent the opinion, research, religious beliefs and scriptural interpretations of the author and not meant to be used in lieu of the advice of ministerial, theological, medical or psychological experts. The novels by Helen Glowacki are works of fiction. References to real people, events, organizations, or locales are intended only to provide a sense of authenticity, and are used fictitiously. Characters, incidents and dialogue are drawn from the author's imagination and are not to be construed as real. Any resemblance to actual persons, living or dead is

The King James Version (KJV) of the Bible, which is public domain in the United States, is used throughout the books by this author. For further study, the author recommends the New King James Version (NKJV) of the Bible as easier reading and less usage of the old world language while remaining true to the original text.

Photography by Roland Edgar Adams

Cape Town, Western Cape, South Africa

FORWARD

From the book *An Attitude to Conquer*
by Daniel Landolfi.

Did you know that God has made us thousands upon thousands of promises? Did you know that you can find all of them in the Bible? Take a moment and think about the many promises from the Bible that you are already aware of and then look at a few of my favorites: *"I can do all things through Christ which strengthen me." "For I am more than a conqueror." " I am the head and not the tail." "I am blessed coming and going." "I am above and not beneath." "I am blessed because God says I am blessed." "I will be of good courage for God will strengthen my heart."*

These are just a handful of the promises which God has made to us, but in order to receive them you must first believe they belong to you.

It says in God's Word in Romans 8:37 that I am more than a conqueror and says in Romans 8:31 that if God is for me, then who can be against me? The Bible also says that everything unclean, every spirit and fowl devil must bow to the name of Jesus Christ (Philippians 2:10), and in Matthew 28:18 it tells us that we have been given the authority to use that name.

The Bible declares that whatsoever I bind on earth is bound in heaven, whatsoever I loose on earth is loosed in heaven (Matthew 16:19) and since these all come directly from the Bible, I believe them 100 percent. Therefore, do you know what kind of attitude I have? A fearless one!

Is God is bigger than all your problems? If you really believe that, then why is it that when things start to happen we believe everything else except that? Jesus healed blind eyes, made the lame walk, commanded limbs to grow, died for the sin of the world, and then rose from the grave three days later.

If He did all this, then do you really think your car payment is out of His grasp? Do you really think that mortgage payment is beyond His abilities? Well….they aren't!

2 Corinthians 4:8-9 tells us: *We are troubled on every side, yet not distressed; we are perplexed, but not in despair; Persecuted, but not forsaken; cast down, but not destroyed.*

The Creator of heaven and earth is your Father. The One who formed a man out of dust… in His image…and breathed life into him loves you and says in Jeremiah 29:11-14: *"For I know the plans I have for you," declares the Lord, "plans to prosper you and not to harm you, plans to give you hope and a future. Then you will call upon me and come and pray to me, and I will listen to you. You will seek me and find me when you seek me with all your heart. I will be found by you"*

That's your Dad!

"One thing have I desired

of the Lord,

that I will seek after;

that I may dwell

in the house of the Lord

all the days of my life,

to behold the beauty of the Lord,

and to enquire in his temple."

Psalm 27: 4

MESSAGE FROM THE AUTHOR

When a child falls from a swing and runs to their parent in tears and in pain, the parent immediately assesses their child's injuries.... and then offers comfort. Only when the parent is assured that the child is in no danger can the parent's fears be allayed. Similarly, when we find ourselves in tears and pain, until we assess what is wrong, and develop the hope that we will be restored we cannot be truly comforted. Knowledge about the circumstances in which we find ourselves is power...self-empowerment. Once we have obtained that knowledge we can assess the risk, make the correct decisions, and begin to work toward whatever healing process we choose.

However, assessing a scraped knee or elbow is very different than assessing a state of mind or attempting to describe the debilitating pain of our fears and our thoughts. Those who are themselves or engage someone who is depressed may not understand what they are experiencing and may not recognize the sadness and the withdrawal caused by emotional suffering. Describing one's depression and why one succumbs to it is incredibly difficult because words which attempt to describe *feelings* are inadequate, thus often defy expression. Describing a sense of abandonment, or rejection, of jealousy or insecurity, fear or hopelessness may not be easily brought to the surface and therefore those with whom one might desire to share those thoughts and feelings often cannot understand the debilitating and exhausting result of such emotion. Further, when the inability to find solace continues long enough, a state of hopelessness can begin to fester, sap the strength required to fight back, and require immediate intervention.

Those who suffer under the scourge of depression, often lose all hope for a recovery thus any admonishment or lack of empathy adds to their sense of isolation and can cause further withdrawal. Thus, gentle understanding and words of love which encourage one's trust in God can better help renew that hope and guide one toward overcoming their circumstances. We must also understand that acknowledging what one may view as a personal failure is not an easy task. Thus when someone is willing to share their story of struggle and what they view as a weakness is a gift of trust. It takes courage to acknowledge failure or weakness and therefore should be a humbling experience for those who are trusted with such an acknowledgement.

The good news is that scripture tells us that God often shines through our weakness and does not look at failure when we desire to change. He wants to lead us away from any path which Satan encourages with the goal of breaking our faith. Thus, it is important that we understand why Satan wants us to be depressed and how God can turn that circumstance into a blessing.

Blaringly absent from most conversations is the recognition that our human nature contains protective devices which insures the survival of our species but which can also work against us. Scripture describes our human nature as the Adam-like nature, and tells us to shed that nature and replace it with a Christ-like nature. This means that we must understand what, or more correctly, *who,* actually instigates our depression and why. Further, and also absent from our conversation is how we can overcome these damaging thoughts and emotions and make the necessary changes. Yet, to learn of God and how our relationship with God plays a major part in overcoming those things which cause us to be unhappy is very important. Finding happiness *despite* our circumstances is not only rewarding, but also the state in which God wants us to live.

Throughout scripture we read that God offers us His protection by describing what we must watch for to protect our physical, emotional and spiritual well-being. Sadly many are unaware that not only has God provided information about our future, but also about how to love one another, how to rebuff attacks from Satan, and how to become the Bride of Christ. Thus few are aware that evil is alive and well and on the attack and that some of these attacks take the form of causing us to feel depressed, isolated, angry and fearful. Nor do they understand why Satan would want to do this. While most of us acknowledge that our life on earth will determine our position in Heaven, few understand that God does not look upon our failures; He looks into our hearts. He sees all things…especially those things which we try to hide from others…. sometimes even from our selves. He understands why we feel as we do and wants to teach us how to change our difficult circumstances and find peace and joy. God teaches us and helps us, so we can learn how much He loves us and through His love, learn how we can truly love.

Scripture expresses God's desire to forgive us for our failures, explain what is required to become an overcomer, and encourage us to draw closer to Him.

He wants us to be found worthy to be with Him and His Son for all eternity. Scripture also teaches us that we have a powerful enemy who wants us to lose our faith and not learn how to move from our Adam-like nature into the Christ-like nature that the Bride God wants for His Son must develop. God wants us to understand that Satan uses those who do not know God's words, or who sin with little or no remorse, to bring harm to the children of God and to give us *reason* to fear or to be depressed. Scripture was, and is the word of God. It is perfect and it is complete. What we learn from scripture can bring us into fellowship with our Heavenly Father, and into the completion necessary to become the Bride of Christ. It can also teach us why we fail and how we can fight those things which bring that failure. It brings us dire warnings about what Satan does, what his powers are and how the fallen angels who left heaven with Satan can invade the soul of mankind. Sadly, few understand this concept and are caught in the subtle traps Satan uses to bring us under his power and into his captivity.

The goal of this book is to explain not only why we feel such powerful emotion, but also why it can be so debilitating… and to explain how God can turn our situation into a blessing. This book is not a substitute for professional or medical support, but to teach about the spiritual side of our struggle and describe the many faces of depression. The more we understand the better equipped we are to obtain the healing we require. Our Heavenly Father is a marvel of love and though we are born sinners, and born with an Adam-like nature which cannot enter the new heaven and earth, God shows us how to be a part of His family and does not give up on us until the last moment. He wants to teach us how we can change our lives; shed the Adam-like nature for a Christ-like nature by learning of Him, of what He asks of us, and how He will help us achieve this goal and be happy in the process. Unfortunately, many challenge scripture and the value of placing our faith in God. They scoff at matters pertaining to faith or religion and view scripture with a closed mind and heart. Yet God wants all men saved and has made equal provision for everyone who ever lived or died to do so. But in the process, God also wants all men to experience peace and happiness despite the circumstances through which they might live. May God bless you and keep you and touch your heart with the desire to learn of Him and be free.

Helen Gumienny Glowacki

"And the Spirit,
and the bride say, Come.
And let him that heareth say, Come,
and let him that is athirst come.
And whosoever will,
let him take the water of life freely."

Revelation 22:17

TABLE OF CONTENTS

Photography by Martin Lansberg
Pietermaritzburg, South Africa

Chapter One

APPEARANCES ARE DECEIVING

Sometimes we drive past a lovely home nestled in a serene setting and landscape, and never guess at the difficult circumstances which might exist behind those walls….nor of the love and understanding the occupants so desperately require. Sometimes we meet people and greet them and never see that they labor under a heavy cross. Even we might be hiding our heartache believing that to share it may place a burden on someone or make us appear less than the impression we wish to create. A friendly greeting and smiling face may hide the pain we feel and therefore, just as we might hide *our* sadness and concerns, others do too. Thus we must learn to be more observant so that we are not so often oblivious to the heartache of others until it is too late. Sadly, the pain and suffering some secretly experience can become so great that it can even take one's life. Learning to be observant about both our own feelings and the feelings of others helps teach us empathy. Experiencing our own heartache is the greatest teacher of all. But when we are unaware of why we go through heartache, or care that others may be suffering, we have no weapon with which to fight; we have no love or understanding of God's plan of salvation.

Being unaware of God's words, of Satan's work, of the joy and responsibility of helping others, can lead to us becoming captive to indifference or captive to any other spirit which Satan sends our way to prevent our worthiness. That captivity can direct not only our feelings, but also our every thought and decision. God however, is fully aware of what Satan can do and the heartache which can result. Throughout scripture God teaches us that He understands our inclinations *and our feelings* and wants to help us. To obtain this help and dramatically change our lives, we must learn what God tells us. Through His words we can learn what to do and how to fight back when we are attacked and also know how to help others when they are attacked. By learning the role Satan plays in our lives and what occurs if we have not placed ourselves under God's protection, we can prepare ourselves to thwart the many forms of captivity Satan uses to trap us.

One of the most important and dramatic verses in the Bible warns of the harm which can come to us when we do not know what we are to watch for and how to fight against that which seeks to harm us. This verse is found in Matthew 12:45 and tells us: *"Then goeth he, and taketh with him seven other spirits more wicked than himself, and they enter in and dwell there; and the last state of that man is worse than the first"*. This statement refers to Satan and the fallen angels who fight with him against

God and God's children, and demonstrates why negative thoughts and actions can escalate.

Scripture teaches us that there is an ongoing war between God and Satan and that we are what the battle is all about. As we begin to understand this spiritual warfare we learn that we must use our free will to choose whether we will fight on the side of good, or remain captive to the side of evil. God wants us to understand that Satan is alive and well and that he operates clandestinely in our lives to break our faith by breaking our bodies and our spirit. There are many avenues through which Satan attacks mankind. Two of his favorite methods are to attack our self-worth to break our faith, or to create an indifferent attitude so we don't reach out to help those in need.

Satan works best when we are not aware of what he does. He does not want us to learn what God teaches us through scripture and wants us to live and die in a state of unawareness. He does not want us to know that our fears and worries, anxieties and hopelessness places us under his captivity and takes away our desire to be close to God and even worse, robs us of our ability to trust God. To break free of this captivity can only be achieved by understanding what Satan does and why.... and how God can change the heartache Satan brings and create a blessing from it. While we alone are ultimately responsible for what we do and feel, God teaches us through scripture that He knows how formidable Satan is and that as long as we strive to overcome, He will help us. Further, that He has provided the forgiveness of sin for those who need time to overcome the traps and pitfalls which Satan brings us. Our battles are rarely won overnight.

Scripture teaches that it is through our hearts attitude, in seeking God's words, desiring to fulfill His admonitions, and hating our failure that God can bless us. Scripture further explains that God, in His perfect righteousness *cannot and will not* allow certain conditions to enter His new kingdom, but has provided both the forgiveness and the help we need to overcome those conditions. Being aware of what scripture tells us can become a great incentive and comfort to those engaged in, yet saddened by their emotions and their reactions to certain stimuli. Those with an understanding of God's words acknowledge that these emotions arise from Satan's work through our Adam-like nature. Our recognition of what is occurring helps us fight those spirits before they become entrenched and thus become more difficult to fight. An attack on our self-esteem can lead to depression, but God's words offer advice about how we can win the battle against Satan's attacks. Scripture also tells us to bear one another's burdens. This means that we are to love and support one another by sharing our struggles and triumphs. Learning how someone else succeeded in fleeing the spirit of depression can be incredibly uplifting….and being supported by someone who understands our struggle is even more rewarding. Sometimes God leads us to professionals who can guide us toward the healing we require.

Sharing experiences with one another helps us to realize that we are not alone and not judged for what we think is a weakness or failure. **Learning of the success of others renews our own hope for success.** Learning who and what is really to blame for our circumstances is amazingly uplifting and thus healing and it also can ease our guilt. Matthew 8:16 explains that there were many who were overcome by Satan in Christ's time and that when Christ cast these spirits out, the people were healed. *"When the evening was come, they brought unto him many that were possessed with devils: and he cast out the spirits with his word, and healed all that were sick."* The keyword here is "healed" and "cast out". Luke 8:29 says, *"(For he had commanded the unclean spirit to come out of the man. For oftentimes it had caught him: and he was kept bound with chains and in fetters; and he brake the bands, and was driven of the devil into the wilderness.)"*

This verse explains that the unclean (ungodly) spirit kept the man bound, and that the devil drove the man to do his bidding. However, through the power of Christ, through prayer and abstaining from those things which the spirit demanded, that spirit could be made to leave. Therefore, both abstinence and God's help to maintain that abstinence, is one of the keys to overcoming these spirits. In terms of depression, this tells us that a spirit of Satan instigates our constantly negative thoughts making us believe that what we fear and experience can never be overcome and that we will never be happy again. By abstaining… meaning that we find a path by which we will not allow those thoughts to remain in our minds….that spirit will eventually leave. That path may be through medication, professional guidance, prayer, scripture or many other single or combined efforts. But when we replace those thoughts with the promises God provides for us, we begin to remember those positive words and…. when we begin to use them automatically…. we begin to trust in them. From that trust, God works His miracles and **we begin to heal because we are no longer "feeding" that**

spirit. The Bible explains that some spirits are more difficult to remove, but by prayer and fasting they can eventually be made to leave. "Fasting" in this context means to "stay away" from, abstain from, the activities these spirits require for their existence. It is the acceptance of the fear and anxiety they place in our hearts which we must rebuke. This occurs when we learn to replace those thoughts with God's promises and follow the path He will provide for us which will lead us to the help we require.

Scripture teaches that when the early apostles complained that they were unable to cast out a certain spirit, Christ told them that only by prayer and 'fasting' could they be cast out. (Matthew 17:21: *"Howbeit this kind goeth not out but by prayer and fasting."* And Mark 9:29 says, *"And he said unto them, This kind can come forth by nothing but by prayer and fasting.")* These verses address the spirits and the authority by which they must leave those they invade. These verses and this manner of healing also address the spirits which cause addictions and can be aptly applied to drug and alcohol and all other addictions as well. However, these verses can also be applied to depression and a host of other captivities which Satan brings to mankind to prevent us from serving, loving and trusting God. Satan uses our failures to keep us captive. But failure does not mean defeat; it means that we need to fight again. **Each time we fight we, in essence, "practice" how to become stronger.** Just as when learning to ride a bicycle, we may need to "practice" one hundred times before we can go it alone and every time we consciously ***strive*** to overcome we weaken that spirit. In time, any spirit seeking to keep us from trusting and following God can be broken and forced to leave. We cannot break this spirit in one single effort and may fall back and fail many times before we finally do overcome. As we said before, Satan is stronger than we are. But God is far stronger than Satan.

However, our initial inability to rise above our debilitating emotions doesn't mean we cannot be forgiven, loved, or nurtured through the process of change, but it does mean that we must never believe that being unhappy is what God wants for His children. Being sad not only affects how we feel, but also affects the lives of those around us. God teaches us to love and never harm others and His words always tell us the truth and always work to bring us into freedom. Freedom under God brings us joy and peace. When we truly believe that God is more powerful than any circumstance; that God loves us and promises to bring us through our difficult circumstances, we will not remain captive to Satan. In fact, often that very circumstance which we have lived through becomes an incredible blessing for us and teaches us empathy for others who suffer. We may be being groomed to become a blessing for others because we did overcome and now have developed the love and compassion to help others in a similar circumstance.

However, if we remain unaware of the power of Satan and the power of his cohorts, or how easily we can become trapped, we cannot understand free will, the choices we are afforded and must make, or the consequences of those choices. If we do not know that Satan instigates our negative thoughts, we may not say "NO" to them. We may instead allow them to implant fear in our hearts. We may never think to ***flee*** from them by immersing ourselves in the fellowship of believers and in God's words. We may forget to replace the negative thoughts with the positive words of God which will weaken that spirit.

Because all of us fall into despair from time to time or into troubled circumstances, God asks us to develop and practice compassion and offer it to others. The world is too dangerous to our spiritual well-being for us not to be armed with God's warnings and promises and not to develop the courage to stand up and fight for the gifts He so freely provides. God's children must exercise love, patience, instruction, and prayer to those who are trapped and help them recognize when Satan attacks and what they can do to fight back. Providing understanding, love, compassion, and prayer brings comfort. Providing exhortations about what God tells us is the path to understanding the role of Satan and how to bypass the traps he lays for us. None of us are free of these attacks though for each of us they come in a different form.

Appearances can be deceiving and those who suffer usually try to hide their pain. But in time, unhappiness, and a heavy heart does reveal itself, and we must look for ways to help even if it is simply by praying for someone we think may be carrying a heavy cross. We must understand that not everyone can easily share the details of their troubles and thus we should simply tell them that we love them; that we are praying for them, and that we offer a trustworthy friendship….and then ***be*** trustworthy!

Those who find themselves depressed should discuss their feelings with their ministers and ask to pray with them. But if depression lingers, professional help might better explain the underlying problem which Satan is employing. Prayer is powerful and God always blesses us when we seek His direction. Fellowship with other believers often brings to light a story which is similar to ours; one which culminated in a wonderful blessing. This inspires those who suffer similar circumstances and gives them hope.

But most importantly, when we are attacked and when we enter into a time of difficulty we must understand that we battle an enemy who is much stronger than we are, and that only with God's help will we defeat this enemy. We cannot isolate ourselves because we are clearly warned in Matthew 12:45: *"Then goeth he, and taketh with him seven other spirits more wicked than himself, and they enter in and dwell there; and the last state of that man is worse than the first".*

NOTES

Photography by Colette van Loggerenberg

Pietermaritzburg, South Africa

Chapter Two

A STEALTHY ATTACK

Scripture tells us that there will be little faith on earth when Christ returns to gather the number of souls God wants for the First Resurrection, and warns that our spiritual destruction will occur because we have not learned and applied God's words. Hosea 4:6 tells us: *"My people are destroyed for a lack of knowledge..."* This lack of knowledge refers to our complacency about learning of God's plan for us, about what He seeks for His new kingdom, and about the work of Satan and the captivity he proposes for us.

As a result, we no longer understand or teach the seriousness and subtlety of the spirits which attack us or why we must overcome them. Yet the fact is that Satan is God's enemy and he is our enemy. And, Satan is stronger than we are and uses his power to thwart God's plan of salvation in order to continue his existence.

Satan knows scripture well and knows God's plan, and he knows when and how his present life will end. He believes that if he can prevent God from obtaining the number of faithful souls God wants by breaking our faith, he will delay the return of Christ and thus delay his fate. Only when we understand evil and the spirits of evil as a daily and insidious threat to our soul, will we survive its onslaught and be properly prepared for Christ's return. Adding to this danger is that our entertainment venues glamorize evil thereby lowering our guard against it.

These entertaining portrayals of evil lull us into dismissing the warnings found throughout scripture which tell us that Satan and his fallen angels walk this earth wielding the power and desire to harm the faith of God's children.

The Bible clearly describes Satan's powers throughout its pages and tells us what Satan can do. It explains that Satan can move men to do his bidding (1 Chronicles 21:1), can walk back and forth on the earth (Job 1:7), can cause illness (Job 2:7), can take God's word from men's hearts (Mark 4:15), can enter man (Luke 22:3 and John 13:27), can blind the minds of them which believe not (2 Corinthians 4:4), can transform himself (2 Corinthians 11:14), can send messengers to hurt man (2 Corinthians 12:7), can hinder people (1 Thessalonians 2:18), can produce signs and has powers (2 Thessalonians 2:9) and uses them to convince us to accept his perversions.

God, however, has given us all the information we need to keep Satan from bringing us harm. Thus we need to learn *what* God tells us and we need to teach this to others so they too can fight against Satan. God has a plan and instituted that plan into the physics of our world for the sole purpose of developing us into the Bride He wants for His Son. He longs to fill His new kingdom with souls who love Him and His Son, *and who love one another*. He wants these souls to value love, integrity, and loyalty, and to practice these attributes voluntarily. Thus God developed a plan of salvation for us and placed it into the physics of our world to encourage each soul to hunger for good by learning about evil. Because God loves us, He helps us find happiness despite what Satan is allowed to do.

God created Adam and Eve as the first souls He hoped would grow in love and loyalty. But when God did this and planned to elevate humans higher than the angels, the angel Lucifer, later known as Satan, rebelled. He was already jealous of Christ, and then also became jealous of mankind when he learned that they were to be elevated above the angels. Satan and those who rebelled with him were thrown to earth knowing they would enter Hell for what they'd done when God's plan was completed. To forestall his end, Satan (Lucifer) destroyed God's relationship with Adam and Eve by enticing them to sin. But God provided a way for Adam and Eve, and the generations to follow, to escape the captivity Satan proposed for them.

Christ offered Himself as the perfect sacrifice by which man's sins could be forgiven. At every turn, Satan interfered with God's plan, trying to break those who followed God, even trying to break Christ so he could forestall his destruction and prolong his freedom. Yet many who are tested by Satan are strengthened through these attacks, and from these souls, God is building what the Bible calls The Bride of Christ. Christ will return at the First Resurrection to take His bride to the wedding feast in Heaven. After the great tribulation which will culminate on earth while they are gone, Christ and those deemed His bride will return to earth to bring testimony during the thousand years of peace when all mankind will accept and return God's love …..because Satan will be bound.

But after one thousand years, Satan will be loosed again so those who newly accepted what God offers them can be tested. Satan will wreak havoc on those not firm in their faith knowing that when the Day of Judgment arrives he will be bound forever. Sadly, those souls who are judged to have willingly spurned God and succumbed to Satan will be cast into hell with Satan, while those who stood firm in their faith will inhabit God's new kingdom where there will be no sorrow, no tears and no evil. Scripture labels those who will be sent to the Lake of Fire with Satan "the goats", while those who will be allowed to enter heaven are termed, "the lambs". Thus everyone, all who were ever born or conceived or died, are caught in this battle and as Satan fights to remain free and powerful, we must fight to remain faithful. Knowledge is power and knowledge of God's words the most powerful.

When we use everything God gives us and do what He asks of us, God terms us an "overcomer" and says in Revelation 3:21: "*...to him that overcometh, will I grant to sit with me in my throne....*" Revelation 7:13-14 says: "*......What are these which are arrayed in white robes?............These are they which came out of great tribulation, and have washed their robes, and made them white in the blood of the Lamb*".

The overcomers will be found worthy to go with Christ at the First Resurrection to become His Bride. Therefore, we must be concerned about our sins and we must seek forgiveness if we hope to be found worthy. Our faults and failings are not as important as our hearts attitude and our striving and true desire to do God's will. Scripture assures us that God forgives us if we are truly repentant and ask for forgiveness. Scripture also tells us that *nothing* is too difficult for God and that *all* heartache can become a blessing. Only those who are taken at the First Resurrection will have their sins totally forgotten and wiped from all record while those who will be judged will have their sins reviewed.

We know from Revelation 7:17 that to be an overcomer isn't easy: *"......and God shall wipe away all tears from their eyes*". We may suffer for a while, but if we stand firm and withstand evil we will grow into an overcomer. Revelation 4:20 says: *"Behold, I stand at the door, and knock; if any man hear my voice, and open the door, I will come in to him, and will sup with him, and he with me."* In Matthew 11:29, God says: *"Take my yoke upon you and learn of me...."* God also warns us to flee evil and says in 1 Timothy 6:11: *"But Thou, O man of God, flee these things; and follow after righteousness, godliness, faith, love, patience, meekness."*

To flee evil we must recognize its subtleties and help our brothers and sisters in faith, and all others to understand the importance of God's words about evil. We must help others recognize how serious this battle is, and to pray for their understanding, acceptance and protection. God helps us and He directs His angels to help us, but He also uses people, from ministers to strangers, to help us and in turn expects us to help others.

As we learn how God looks after us, we must be willing to look after others, and teach others that *every* day we enter into a fierce battle against a formidable enemy who wants to thwart God's plan. God will help us, but when we know His words, we are better equipped to use His help and offer it to those we love. But to do this we must have a true relationship with God.

Some believe that attending church, believing that Christ died for us, and being "good people" automatically provides us with a true relationship with God. While these are commendable, they do not provide the relationship God longs to have with us, nor is it enough for the Bride of His Son. What then is a good relationship? Revelation 3:15–16 warns: *"I know thy works, that thou art neither cold nor hot: I would thou wert cold or hot. So then because thou art lukewarm, and neither cold nor hot, I will spue thee out of my mouth."*

When we first fall in love, we care so much for the one we love that we devise many ways to demonstrate our love. We also communicate intimately with the one we love which allows us to be entwined in heart and mind and spirit. We would be like-minded. We would appreciate one another and express that appreciation. This is what would keep us close. We would articulate our love for one another and share our triumphs and our burdens with one another.

Thus we must ask ourselves if we converse with God as we do with those we love and do we do this many times each day? Do we speak to God of our difficulties and our triumphs as we would with our loved one? Do we trust God and ask His advice as we would with the one with whom we share our temporal life? Do we seek to do little things every day to show God how much we love him as we do with the person we fell in love with? Do we make an effort to learn what pleases God as we did the one with whom we fell in love? If we do not do the things which all good relationships require we haven't yet developed the relationship with God which allows Him full entry into our hearts and minds, into our spirit and our future. And if we haven't yet developed that relationship, we really don't know Him.

God wants to develop a bride for His Son, and inhabitants for His new heaven and new earth. He wants those who will desire to give and show love. Each of us must learn what love really is and begin by helping and encouraging one another. Love is the trust with which we describe our worries to our Heavenly Father and ask Him to guide us, trusting that He will. Love is the intimacy through which we ask Him to bless us and teach us and protect us every day. Love is having the courage to stand firm and fight to retain the values and treasures He has given us. Love is putting the welfare of others before our own. This, along with our repentance, our tithing and effort, our willingness to learn His words and to help others, will result in a true relationship of love and trust. And when our hearts are moved, and our eyes fill with thankful tears for the love God gives us, and our goal is to strive to be an overcomer, we know that we have finally allowed God to touch our hearts and that we have touched His.

That is a relationship with God, but it is also the guarantee that God is always at our side and will never let anything happen to us that He will not turn into a blessing for us. However none of this can occur if we do not know God's words and do not recognize that Satan plans a stealthy attack on every child of God in an effort to break their faith. We cannot fight what we cannot recognize and we cannot overcome without God's help.

God understands the evil which plots to break the faith of His children. Thus He has sent us the Holy Spirit which comforts us and which also warns us of danger. When we love God and actively seek Him there is nothing He won't do within His parameters of righteousness to watch over us and provide for us. Despite the stealthy attacks from Satan and his cohorts, we are provided with a way to recognize danger and learn what we can do to protect ourselves. As our hearts open to God, our heart also opens to the Holy Spirit and we learn to listen to or sense its admonitions and direction.

As we are drawn to God and learn what He tells us in scripture, we learn what He recommends we do not only to protect our lives from the work of Satan, but to learn how to completely trust God. We easily accept that we are required to obtain a passport to enter another country, yet seem unable to accept that we will be required to meet certain requirements to enter Heaven.

The sacraments of Holy Baptism, of Holy Communion and of Holy Sealing are the *basic* requirements we must meet. Baptism is a covenant we enter with God whereby we are given the help to break Satan's hold on us through the sin of Adam and Eve. Holy Communion forgives those sins *for which we have remorse, which we hate to commit, and for which we agree to strive not to repeat.* Holy Sealing is the invitation we provide to the Holy Spirit to come and dwell with us and for which we work to provide a holy habitat in our bodies. These are performed by an Apostle of Christ who has been given the authority to provide these sacraments.

Armed with these sacraments and what God wants us to know about His plan of salvation and the spiritual war in which we are engaged helps us understand what we face and why it is worth the battle. Additionally armed with the Holy Spirit to guide us, we will always be led to whatever help we require.

NOTES

Photography by Colette van Loggerenberg

Pietermaritzburg, South Africa

Chapter Three

SIGNS OF TROUBLE

Once we understand the role of Satan and are armed with what the sacraments provide for us, we know what to look for and what steps we can take to fight against the captivity Satan proposes for us. Satan brings all kinds of heartache. It sometimes comes quickly and all at once and other times it creeps slowly into our lives. Sometimes we are not even aware of how sad or fearful we are or how complacent or accepting we have become until its signs and symptoms become quite severe. These methods of attack catch us unaware and we are often unprepared to fight and our emotions begin to rule our thoughts. Sadly, once our thoughts become negative and ingrained they are difficult to fight and as we try and then fail to overcome we feel guilty.

We know that we should not allow any emotion to reign in our hearts or thoughts which robs us of our strength and energy, negatively affects our loved ones, holds us back from thankfulness or damages our faith in God. Thus, having these emotions adds guilt to the mix and guilt in itself is debilitating and can cause us to give in to a sense of unworthiness and lose our self-esteem.

In fact one of the most difficult things for a truly loving child of God to learn is how to forgive themselves. While they easily forgive others, mistakes made while fighting heartache or mistakes made in earlier in life often come back to our thoughts and, through guilt cause sleepless nights and anguish. Satan brings those thoughts.

Retracting past actions, feelings and words is not possible and Satan can replay these in our minds making us wish that those circumstances had not occurred.

Satan uses our guilt to keep us from turning to God and believing that God will forgive us and heal us. Satan uses our misplaced guilt against us even though we know that Christ died for our sins and that His death was the perfect sacrifice through which our sins were not only forgiven but wiped from all record spiritually. If scripture teaches us these truths and if we believe what scripture tells us, then we know that our continued guilt and anguish originates from Satan and is not brought by God.

Once we clearly accept and understand that these thoughts originate from Satan's work in our heart and mind, we know that through God, we can overcome them. We must first recognize that Satan's job is to destroy our faith and stop us from following the direction God wants to give us so we can be healed. Satan believes that by doing this he can prolong his freedom.

To destroy our faith requires an attack on our hope, our courage, and our ability to trust what God has promised. If Satan can successfully attack us on these fronts, he may break an otherwise strong faith. If he can cause us to be negative, filled with guilt, tired, exhausted from our thoughts of the past, or filled with fear about our future, he can wear us down. We need, then to ask ourselves why Satan would have this power over us and what we need to do to thwart such a spiritual attack. Christ provides one of the most wonderful offers to counteract this problem in John 14:27 where He says, *"Peace I leave with you, my peace I give unto you: not as the world giveth, give I unto you. Let not your heart be troubled, neither let it be afraid."* This is very powerful. What these words tell us is that when we pray, we can thank God for the peace He has provided for us, and remind Him that both He and Christ promised that we could not only keep what peace we can muster from within ourselves, but that we can also have the peace They willingly offer us. We can ask for this in our prayers and ask that it work to still our troubled heart and mind. This can be incredibly effective because having peace over our concerns allows us to think and act more rationally, thus more positively.

However, if this approach is not sufficient, then we need to take a good look at ourselves so we can search for what might be holding us back from finding that peace. If we have asked for forgiveness from God, if we are truly remorseful, if we are striving to overcome those tendencies, and if we have partaken of Holy Communion… and still have no peace, then we must look inward. Satan has looked into our heart and found something which he is using to his advantage. 2 Corinthians 2:11 warns: *"Lest Satan get an advantage"*.

Many of us are perfectionists. We work hard and push ourselves to perform at a high level of achievement. This can be a very good trait. However, sometimes the gifts we have been given which allow us to perform at this level become mixed with pride. We are proud of our achievements and proud of the hard work we willingly placed into those achievements. But pride has no place in the life of a child of God. God has said in Proverbs 29:23, "*A man's pride shall bring him low....*" And 1 John 2:16 tell us, "*For all that is in the world, the lust of the flesh, and the lust of the eyes, and pride of life, is not of the Father, but is of the world.*" Pride comes from Satan and can easily cause us to put so much of ourselves into our achievements that we no longer take time for God. We no longer value our spiritual development and the Christ-like nature that we are to develop, but instead value the material and temporal or the Adam-like nature God wants us to overcome. We begin to believe that it is our personal effort which created the achievement rather than God's blessing. **Loving the achievement excessively can be devastating if it is taken from us.** This is what

God means when He tells us that it is easier for a camel to go through the eye of a needle than for a rich man to enter heaven. "Riches" come in many forms and these verses do not refer just to money but to everything we value if we value it more than we value God.

When we have great pride we also begin to view ourselves as exceptional and want others to do the same. Thus when we are forced to admit that we have not been perfect in the eyes of God or the eyes of our peers, our pride is hurt and subconsciously this creates the need to feel good again about ourselves. This need causes us to enter into a never ending cycle of thoughts which are made up of fear, guilt and concern about our personal failures and can even spawn jealousy for what others have. Rather than keep us humble this makes us angry at the situation which we think "forced" us to become imperfect. Satan wants these emotions to create a barrier to the love, protection and forgiveness of our Heavenly Father and a barrier to us having a humble and trusting heart. A blow to our pride is often what hurts so much when we experience a loss such as the loss of a prestigious job or our health or even when a divorce occurs which we did not want. The sadness we feel is a mixture of grief and a mixture of the blow it is to our pride. Rather than think of it as an opportunity for a better life, we rail against what we perceive a loss and ask God to give it back to us. It is difficult under these circumstances to thank God for what has occurred and to trust that He knows what is best for us. It is difficult to believe that what has occurred is for our good. We should view it as an opportunity to grow in faith and to move to a better place spiritually and physically.

Dwelling on the hurt caused by a broken relationship not only exacerbates our emotional and physical pain, but it also brings a great deal of guilt, anger and distrust which then compounds one's pain. While it is necessary to move on and to remain positive, we must dispassionately examine the underlying causes for the broken relationship. We need to learn if there is something which we need to know which could help us avoid a repeat of the situation in the future. To do this we must begin to understand and recognize the Adam-like nature of man which is a selfish, disobedient and indiscriminate nature existing in all of us and must be recognized and overcome so we can build better future relationships through a Christ-like nature.

To alleviate the pain of a perceived loss **one must forgive but carefully consider and remember what to avoid in the future.** God wants us to forgive, but has *not* asked us to forget the protective measure which this learning experience might offer us. Our Heavenly Father may have allowed a broken relationship in our lives to create a better and wiser person of us for the future, or to protect us from a relationship which would have harmed our spiritual life. Thus we must bring the problem to God and then trust Him to direct our lives as He sees fit. Satan uses people to harm people. Some of these people are good people who fall prey to the mistakes Satan inspires. Others are not concerned about what God wants of them. Therefore we need to employ the power of the Holy Spirit to discern what lives in our heart *and* in the heart of others so we can flee those situations in the future.

Evil circles and tempts, thus **remembering the lessons attached to our mistakes, as well as the mistakes of others, warns us not to engage the spirits attached to them again.** Further, if our relationships are with souls who do not seek God, we become unequally yoked whereby one or both who share that yoke will inevitably fall.

We each have a responsibility to be prudent, and to be aware of evil, and to 'watch'. 1 Peter 4:7 tells us, *"But the end of all things is at hand; be ye therefore sober, and watch unto prayer."* 1 Peter 5:8 says, *"Be sober, be vigilant, because your adversary the devil, as a roaring lion, walketh about, seeking who he may devour."* We cannot watch, nor be vigilant if we forget our lessons or if we never grow from them. Life is the training ground; the childhood of those who God wants to mature into a bride for His Son. Therefore our lessons are *necessary* to placing us on the correct path. However, once we have learned to watch for the spirit of pride or any other spirit seeking to entrap us, to acknowledge that all we have comes from God and not through our own achievement, and that we can trust God, we can overcome. We can free ourselves of the pride, anger, guilt and distrust which creates the inability to forgive ourselves and to let go and let God.

Allowing God to direct our lives means that we are learning to trust Him and we are accepting the multitude of lessons which come out of our struggles. We can be thankful that God so patiently brings us into an awareness of those things which we need to address so we can grow into the bride He wants for His Son. **We can then begin to see how a blessing is created from our heartache**. When Scripture teaches us to arm ourselves with the word of God it does so to help us learn of the spiritual wickedness which seeks to devour us. The armor scripture speaks of is God's words, His instruction, and His protection. When our heart is right with God and we fully understand what He asks of us, what dangers we face, and what our future will be, and we strive to please Him, we will have His guidance and protection.

Once we learn how to develop the wisdom, courage and self-esteem to overcome, to seek others willing to do the same, we will have matured enough to have something of value to offer. But if we remain complacent in godly matters, desperate in personal need, and without introspection, empathy, or trust we cannot grow and may make the same painful mistakes over and over again. Thus we must learn how to forgive…both ourselves and others. We must say no to thoughts which bring fear and anger. We must watch for pride and a lack of peace. We must examine whether or not we are equally yoked with those around us so we can learn God's ways and practice them freely. We must watch for all things evil and bring our concerns to God. But the bottom line is that we learn to trust God in every circumstance. If we can do this, we will win over the spirits which want to bring us harm. **It is through our trust in God that fear cannot touch us and the future cannot make us tremble.**

The end times are a dangerous era for all children of God. It is a time of great power for Satan. If we are not spiritually prepared, Satan's anger and desperation can bring us harm not only spiritually, but also emotionally, and physically. Thus **we must remember and learn just as we must forgive. We must be watchful and discerning just as we are loving and kind.** We must not let our guard down as these end times envelop us and **we must remember that God loves us.**

The struggles we encounter and the sadness these struggles bring show themselves differently in different people. Some become quiet and reserved. Some withdraw from interaction with others. Some consistently express anger over their life circumstances. Some are bitter and others simply cry in hopelessness. As children of God we should look for these signs in others so we can offer more love and support and become a role model for them. To do so however also requires that when we offer our hand in love and friendship that we do so with integrity. **Friendship is a gift not to be dishonored by gossip or envy, but honored by empathy and love, by forgiveness and *constancy.***

God measures how we befriend others to see how we will behave in His family… with Him…. with His Son…. and with those They love.

When we watch for all these markers in ourselves and in others we will be better armed to fight Satan and garner God's help. Satan is never blatant, but works behind the scenes, hiding his work until we are trapped by it.

NOTES

Photography by Anthony Hicks
Cape Town, Western Cape, South Africa

Chapter Four

WHY DOES FELLOWSHIP HELP?

One of the most wonderful gifts God has provided for His children is the comfort of others who share their faith. In Galatians 6:2, the Apostle Paul told his congregations to *"Bear ye one another's burdens, and so fulfil the law of Christ"*. And in Galatians 6:6, he said, *"Let him that is taught in the word communicate unto him that teacheth in all good things."* These words coupled with words such as fellowship, friend, fellowservant, fellowsoldier, fellowworker, fellowdisciple, and fellowlabourer indicate the bond which God's children should share with one another, and the love toward one another which should emanate to and from them.

Fellowship is defined by Webster's dictionary as "companionship", and "the company of equals". This describes a kind of kinship or friendship which God encourages among believers. **What we surround ourselves with will leave its mark on us.** Because we are so easily influenced by our surroundings, God warns us not to have fellowship with evil but with good.

As the Apostles traveled from city to city to bring the gospel to others, God told them to search for someone they knew, someone in their congregation of believers who resided in the city to which they traveled. If they found no one and were to preach to those they wished to convert, God told them that He would choose someone in that city who would help them and believe in their cause. The Apostles enjoyed being with believers, but also enjoyed being with new converts because in such a group they felt safe, comfortable and comforted. They could trust! God wants no less for us.

Our Heavenly Father knows that when we are tired, or overburdened, or if we feel defeated, those who *truly* share our faith will help us and uplift us. Those who love God can pray together, and break bread together as the Apostles did. It is this joyous spiritual comfort which encourages the children of God to have fellowship with one another. But it is also because we can find godly advice in this circle as well as any admonition we may require.

Sometimes we don't recognize when our path is a dangerous one. We don't see the work of Satan in our lives. But in fellowship with other believers, those who do recognize this danger can remind us of what Ephesians 5:11 says: *"And have no fellowship with the unfruitful works of darkness, but rather reprove them."* It is also comforting to know that when we do make a mistake we are forgiven, encouraged, and still loved and welcome in the circle of believers, even when we must be warned that our path might need correction.

Fellowship with other believers should be an important factor in the life of a child of God. We are not pulled in two directions when we are like-minded and cognizant of how God wants us to behave. Our conversations will often be about our faith or how we can help those in need. What we seek to understand of scripture can also be revealed to us as we share conversation with believers. When one is weak in faith others can provide strength, when one lacks understanding others can teach, when one is weary, another will uplift. The hand of friendship we receive, and the trust we can obtain through those friendships is precious. The conversations and the role models we are given bring us consolation, comfort, instruction, and love. Philippians 2:1 tells us, *"If there be therefore any consolation in Christ, if any comfort of love, if any fellowship of the Spirit……"*

If we have never been offered the hand of friendship from those in our congregation then we should extend our own hand. Galatians 2:9 gives us this example: *"….they gave to me and Barnabas the right hand of fellowship; that we should go unto the heathen….."* As children of God we will find a blessing in imitating the actions of the Apostles which are revealed in scripture. As an example, in Acts 2:42, we are told: *"And they continued stedfast in the apostle's doctrine and fellowship, and in breaking of bread, and in prayers."* And in Colossians 4:11, *"……….These only are my fellowworkers unto the kingdom of God, which have been a comfort unto me."*

Sometimes, however, despite our good intentions, Satan blocks our desire for a godly, learning experience and seeks to block us from finding souls who are like-minded. Sadly, many congregations have a member or two who never see the beam in their eye but always point out the speck in others. Their pride, arrogance, self-importance and judgmental attitude prevent us from trusting them. Perhaps they speak the loudest and longest and not only dominate conversations and activities, but also dominate the decisions and conclusion of all discussions and we no longer have a part to play. It may also be that sarcasm, jealousy, venom or threats, based on feelings or emotion, rather than on sound principles are expressed and push us into our shell preventing us from sharing and learning God's words and ways. Those who perpetrate these activities carry power from Satan and use that power to intimidate, rather than teach, discuss or uplift.

Thus the child of God is faced with the dilemma of seeing this approach gain power and influence and thus feeling and experiencing a great personal weakness when trying to right the situation. So what should the child of God do to gain confidence and approach a situation where one appears much stronger than the other? How can one effect the change one desires and knows to be the more godly approach?

The answer is two-fold. One is to pray and the other is to know what God tells us to do and to trust…to have faith… that following God's directives will bring results. What we must understand is that God *enjoys* demonstrating His love, His protection and His power to His children and He enjoys working through *weakness* to prove His power and protection to both the true believer and the unbeliever and even to the Pharisee-like believer.

1 Corinthians 1:27 tells us, *"But God hath chosen the foolish things of this world to confound the wise; and God hath chosen the weak things of the world to confound the things which are mighty."* Even the Apostle Paul acknowledged that God worked through the weakness which the Apostle

wished he could change. Paul said in 11 Corinthians 12:10: *"Therefore I take pleasure in infirmities, in reproaches, in necessities, in persecutions, in distresses for Christ's sake, for when I am weak, then I am strong."* And in the prior verse, 11 Corinthians 12:9 he said, *".....for my strength is made perfect in weakness."*

Further, 1 Corinthians 2:3 says: *"And I was with you in weakness, and in fear, and in much trembling."* Throughout scripture we find that God clearly tells us that He will always be with us when we need Him. Job 39:11-12 says, *"Wilt thou trust him, because his strength is great? Or wilt thou leave thy labor to him? Wilt thou believe him that he will bring home thy seed, and gather it into thy barn?"*

In Malachi 3:10 God says, *"And prove me now herewith, saith the LORD of hosts, if I will not open you the windows of heaven, and pour you out for you a blessing that there shall not be room enough to receive it."* In Psalm 91:15-16, God promises, *"He shall call upon me, and I will answer him; I will be with him in trouble; I will deliver him, and honour him"*. Psalm 27:1 tells us, *"The lord is my light and my salvation; whom shall I fear?....."* Jeremiah 33:3 promises, *"Call unto me, and I will answer thee....."* Isaiah 43:2 tells us, *"When thou passeth through the waters, I will be with you......"*

And Hebrews 13:5 says, *"For he hath said, I will never leave you nor forsake thee."* Further, Titus 2:1 says *"But speak thou the things which become sound doctrine."* 11 Timothy 2:16 states, *"All scripture is given by inspiration of God, and is profitable for doctrine, for reproof, for correction, for instruction in righteousness"*. And 11 Timothy 4:2 instructs, *"Preach the word; be instant in season, out of season; reprove, rebuke, exhort with all longsuffering...."* These verses clearly tell us to learn God's words and then speak them boldly and with conviction to correct and to exhort.

Scripture also tells us to have faith that God will be at our side, loving us, and protecting us when we apply His words, and that we are to have no fear when doing so. We also learn that even if we see no immediate result from what we have said and done, God is working behind the scenes, using our words, our courage, and our faith to bring about a miracle. He is protecting us from the wiles of Satan as well. Even when there seems little hope because of our meekness, our longsuffering, and our forgiving hearts, yet we have spoken boldly of God's words and we have faith, God will always step in to give us the victory even if it is not immediately recognized. *Satan can be beaten by our trust in God despite our weaknesses* or vulnerability.

Sadly, many give lip service to God yet have no understanding of God's Plan of Salvation, no understanding of how Satan works and no knowledge of scripture. Nor do they have love to give. Others may be aware of these things yet are blinded by Satan to their own failings. Sometimes we have to be patient and let God work these things out. Often He allows his wayward children time to see the error of their ways....thus our patience is required as that takes place. Perhaps, if we have done our best and failed, it is time to let go and let God and bring our concerns to God asking Him to help us connect with like-minded children of God so we can find the comfort and love we seek and leave the others to their own resources.

While scripture teaches us to rebuke and exhort one another, scripture also tells us to be gentle in how we speak to one another, to not provoke one another to anger, and to love one another. It teaches that we are to draw others through our example and not by contentious debate. Many are won by our honor and integrity and through love thus while we can quote scripture to make a point, we must be careful that we do not appear to be judgmental. The Bible also reminds us (in Mark 10:27) that what is impossible for man is possible for God, thus if we do not appear to make an impact on those who do cause contention, God can make an impact.

Prayer can also move God to perform the impossible both for the individual and those for whom they pray. Thus praying for others is something we should always do and something in which we can place our faith. Praying gives us greater power and keeps Satan at bay. However, **knowing when to withdraw from someone, coupled with our continued kindness, patience and prayer, and sometimes....quiet.... will allow love to be the victor.** More importantly, this approach will leave another day for *fruitful* testimony...perhaps even by someone else.

Our Heavenly Father works to open all hearts, wants all men to be saved, and only He truly knows what lives in someone's heart. Being meek, or shy, quiet or even weak demonstrates a lack of pride and a lack of pretentiousness and these allow God to become the driver of a conversation and a deed.

The Holy Spirit can then speak rather than the person and gives strength and power to that person's words and actions. God loves to prove Himself and can do so easily in those who allow His power to govern their lives. Further, Satan is thwarted by love and by our lack of anger despite what he brings to any debate, action or conversation. Knowing that it is Satan who brings our heartache and that God allows it because He will use it to bring us a blessing is inspiring and helps us cope. Knowing this allows us to wait in patience and trust that no harm will come to us.

Even Christ needed and sought the fellowship of those whom He trusted when he felt depressed and tired. He often chose to travel to Bethany where he could visit with Mary and Martha and Lazarus who were his personal friends. He also spent time with His disciples and Apostles rather than be alone with His thoughts. Christ needed people and so do we. Christ was often disappointed in those He loved…so are we. But with God's help, with prayer, and with the discernment of the Holy

Spirit we will find those with whom we are equally yoked…..those who will love us.

As mentioned above, in Malachi 3:10 God says, *"And prove me now herewith, saith the LORD of hosts, if I will not open you the windows of heaven, and pour you out for you a blessing that there shall not be room enough to receive it."* And in 1 Corinthians 2:3 *"And I was with you in weakness, and in fear, and in much trembling."*

NOTES

Photography by Janet Reeds Lourens

Johannesburg, South Africa

Chapter Five

WHY WE FEEL SAD

Deep in the heart and soul of the true children of God is the desire to do as God asks, to seek the kingdom of heaven, and to be a part of the bride of Christ. That's a huge undertaking and if we are humble, truly humble we cannot be absolutely sure that we have really done all we can to meet those goals. This alone can make us sad.... but it is a sign of our humbleness rather than a sign of depression or pride or arrogance. This type of sadness makes us wake up each morning hoping to do better and to take Holy Communion with a greater desire to overcome. When we are this humble, and open to seeking God's will for our lives, when something does not sit quite right in our heart and soul, we feel it. We know that something is not right. We feel an underlying anxiety and a nagging sadness as the Holy Spirit tries to tell us what we need to do or to avoid so we can correct or protect our path. Whether it is an argument with our spouse or child, a lack of trust that God will help our current need, a "little white lie", or a wave of jealousy, the true child of God knows that they have grieved the Holy Spirit within them, thus they feel sad, sometimes even a sense of anxiety. But there is a difference between this type of sadness and depression.

This type of sadness will fade immediately when we right the wrong or we seek Holy Communion whereas depression hangs on and defies even one happy moment. Depression contains fear and is not relieved by taking Holy Communion. Depression requires that we slowly develop a greater trust in God for *every* circumstance, allow His will over our own will by allowing Him to direct us to the help we require. Without that trust we cannot be healed and cannot be an overcomer. Sometimes, God leads us to professional help whereby we can pray and ask Him to give godly wisdom to those to whom we go for help. Either way, the goal is simply to be healed and to overcome.

God has promised us as written in Revelation 21:7, *"He that overcometh shall inherit all things; and I will be his God, and he will be my son."* To understand who will be a part of the First Resurrection and therefore be an overcomer, we are given an analogy in scripture that the overcomers are those who accepted an invitation to a wedding feast **and prepared for that feast.** Revelation 19:7-8 explains, *"Let us be glad and rejoice, and give honour to him; for the marriage of the Lamb is come, and his wife hath made herself ready."* Scripture provides a number of parables which address this subject; one of which is when Christ described a wedding feast as an analogy to those who would be gathered at the First Resurrection. Christ warned that those who were originally bidden to attend the wedding would not accept the invitation and therefore the invitation was extended to others. Matthew 22:9 tells us, *"Go ye therefore into the highways and as many as ye shall find, bid to the marriage."* Then, in Matthew 2:10 we learn, *"So those servants went out into the highways, and gathered together all as many as they found, both bad and good: and the wedding was furnished with guests."* The parable ends with the words from Matthew 22:14, *"For many are called, but few are chosen."* This tells us that our place may be given to someone else!

When we search further in scripture we find the parable of the five foolish and the five wise virgins. Matthew 25:10 tells us, *"And when they went to buy, the bridegroom came; and they that were ready went in with him to the marriage; and the door was shut."* This verse tells us that the five foolish virgins had not properly prepared and ran quickly to purchase what was required, but when they returned they found the door shut and they could not participate. In these verses we are being asked to "prepare". The word prepare indicates that work is necessary to complete this chore. Yet, when we are depressed we become lethargic and we lose the energy we need to tackle that work. Therefore we must overcome the depression.

Revelation 7:13 explains, *"And one of the elders answered, saying unto me, What are these which are arrayed in white robes? And whence came they?"* Revelation 7:14 answers saying, *".....And he said to me, These are they which came out of great tribulation, and have washed their robes, and made them white in the blood of the Lamb."* And in Revelation 7:16-17 we learn, "*They shall hunger no more, neither thirst any more, neither shall the sun light on them, nor any heat. For the Lamb which is in the midst of the throne shall feed them, and shall lead them unto living fountains of waters; and God shall wipe away all tears from their eyes."*

These verses sum up what is required for the transformation which must take place for us to be included in the wedding feast. We must be "arrayed" and must "wash" our robes despite our tribulations. These are verbs and verbs require action. The words: "overcomer" and "white robe" require that we be transformed in word and deed by learning and doing God's words and by being faithful to God. It is however not always easy to recognize the progress of a child of God because the changes we make are often slowly achieved. These may include the curbing of anger, increasing tithes to ten percent, a strong prayer life, laying aside secret sins, and loving and trusting God. Through these efforts, a transformation is taking place. Looking back over a period of time demonstrates those changes and demonstrates the ***striving*** which God looks for.

1 Peter 1:22 tells us, *"Seeing ye have purified your souls in obeying the truth through the Spirit unto*

unfeigned love..., by the word of God....." And in 1 Peter 2:9, "*But ye are a chosen generation, a royal priesthood, an holy nation, a peculiar people; that ye should shew forth the praises of him who hath called you out of darkness into his marvelous light.*" And 1 Peter 2:25 sums it up by saying, "*For ye were as sheep going astray; but are now returned unto the Shepherd and Bishop of your souls.*" And James 4:7, "*Submit yourselves therefore to God. Resist the devil, and he will flee from you.*" Romans 12:1-2 clearly assures us, "*I beseech you therefore, brethren, by the mercies of God, that ye present your bodies a living sacrifice, holy, acceptable unto God, which is your reasonable service. And be not conformed to this world; but be ye transformed by the renewing of your mind; that ye may prove what is that good, and acceptable, and perfect, will of God.*"

However, Satan wants us to feel shame and exhaustion, sadness and lethargy so that we lose our faith when we do not live up to these expectations.

He does not want us to ***believe that God forgives our sins and forgets them when we repent and strive to do better.*** By keeping us captive to our failures, Satan prolongs his freedom. He knows what the Bible says and knows that God wants a certain number of souls to be ready when He sends His Son back to earth. Thus **Satan works diligently to prevent the transformation from child of God to Bride of Christ** and specifically attacks us through guilt and repeated failure.

Our inability to do what God expects of us makes us both sad and angry and can cause us to forget that **God looks at our striving rather than our failures**. God wants us to acknowledge our sin, hate our sin, to feel remorse for our sins and to desire to do better in the future. This can be achieved only when we truly know and love God. This is why our Heavenly Father wants us to learn His words from scripture. He provides us with information about our future. He understands that as the end times are fulfilled Satan will attack more vehemently, that we will persecuted, and that evil will prosper, thus God wants us to be assured that He will care for us in all things if we remain faithful.

By understanding God's plan of salvation and what He offers, and knowing that our suffering is for a limited time, and our mistakes forgiven, we can withstand the days of evil and the wiles of Satan. We can overcome our troubles because we know what we are striving for and why we are attacked. We know that God will help us and that our troubles are but for a little while ….as opposed to an eternity as the Bride of Christ. God wants us to understand death and the torment that death and the second death brings to sinners. He wants us to know of the hope and joy He offers to those who strive to be His children and for whom natural death is not the end. None of us will escape death, but the children of God will escape the second death.

Those who remain faithful to God and humbly seek to have their sins forgiven will receive rewards which are so great that they are beyond description. Thus God provides us, through scripture, with a glimpse of the new heaven and earth to strengthened us and show us what He wants to give us. The Apostle John, while on the island of Patmos and inspired by the Holy Spirit, wrote many descriptive passages about the new Heaven and Earth. For example, John spoke about streets paved in gold as an analogy to help us comprehend the immense beauty of the City of God which those who remain faithful will enjoy. God calls those who will be given these gifts His firstfruits and while others may enter heaven, this group will live and reign at God's side as the Bride of Christ who are the overcomers and will be the kings and priests of His new world.

The information God provides for His children through scripture includes a description of what happens after death. Scripture explains that when

Christ returns we will be given a celestial body which will never know sickness, sorrow, or death. 1 Corinthians 15:35 says, *"But some man will say, How are the dead raised up? and with what body do they come? Behold, I shew you a mystery;* and 1 Corinthians 15:51 tells us, *"We shall not all sleep, but we shall all be changed."*

These verses tell us that all men must die, but that those who follow Christ will be made alive and will be changed. When we rise again after death we will be transformed from a terrestrial or natural body to a celestial or spiritual body. 1 Corinthians 15:40 tells us, "*There are also celestial bodies, and bodies terrestrial: but the glory of the celestial is one, and the glory of the terrestrial is another."* And 1 Corinthians 15:44 says, *"It is sown a natural body; it is raised a spiritual body. There is a natural body, and there is a spiritual body."* This is an incredible promise and revelation, but there is also a warning which tells us that we must labor for this gift by being faithful, and by striving to learn and do as God asks.

1 Corinthians 15:58 tells us, "*Therefore, my beloved brethren, be ye steadfast, unmoveable, always abounding in the work of the Lord, forasmuch as ye know that your labour is not in vain of the Lord.*" Psalm 1:1-3 tells us, "*Blessed is the man that walketh not in the counsel of the ungodly, nor standeth in the way of sinners, nor sitteth in the seat of the scornful. But his delight is in the law of the Lord; and in his law doth he meditate day and night. And he shall be like a tree planted by the rivers of water, that bringeth forth his fruit in his season; his leaf also shall not wither, and whatsoever he doeth shall prosper.*" Here we learn who God will bless and thus what our behavior must be to be worthy of the celestial body which will rise at the First Resurrection.

The children of God await the return of Christ who will take from the earth those who are worthy to become His Bride. The children of God understand that God seeks a bride for His Son who is filled with the desire and ability to love. Thus, God's children ***strive*** to overcome their self-serving Adam-like nature and develop a Christ-like nature to achieve this goal.

They understand that a loving father who seeks a bride for his son would want that bride to be kind, longsuffering, and forgiving. They also know that scripture warns that perhaps only half of those who are believers will meet the criteria required to become the Bride. **The five foolish virgins were believers,** but were not prepared for the arrival of the bridegroom, thus not allowed to go with Christ when He came for them. (Matthew 1:1-13, and 24:40-41)

To become a part of the Bride of Christ is the hope of all the true and striving children of God and requires work to develop the Christ-like and gentle nature of love and goodness, and the desire to spurn all things evil. A strong and unfailing faith along with a loving heart and the effort to be pleasing in the eyes of God is absolutely necessary and therefore not all who believe will be found worthy to become the Bride of Christ, even though our Heavenly Father longs for all men to be saved. Thus He helps us, He loves us and He forgives us if we learn to love, try our best and trust Him.

As mentioned earlier, for those not found worthy to be a part of the Bride, there will be judgment day when each will be judged based upon their faith and ***all*** past deeds. Those deemed the lambs will be allowed to enter heaven, but not the City of God where the family of God will reside. The goats who allowed sin and hatred, anger and a lack of faith and love to govern their lives will be sent to the Lake of Fire for the second death where they will be in torment for all eternity. Thus, though not all are called to be the Bride, many will be a part of the kingdom of God. However, many will be cast into the Lake of Fire with Satan to experience the second death. The second death is separation from God and from love for all eternity. There is no redemption from the second death, it is torment; it is life surrounded only with evil and it is for all eternity; it is forever.

These words may seem harsh but are a reminder that **not all believers will be a part of the First Resurrection** and become a part of the Bride of Christ and thus the family of God. We need to strive to shed our old nature, become more like Christ, desire to leave all things evil and learn to love. Really love.

God knows our motives and our faults and failings. But He also knows our striving and hears our prayers to love more, and to grow in compassion. The Bride of Christ will be expected to be perfect in her love toward others. She must personify love by being, applying, developing, teaching, and giving love. When we truly love, we automatically desire to spurn what is not righteous in the eyes of God and long to be with Him for all eternity where love will reign and evil will not exist. And often…..what we have suffered here on earth was what gave us the compassion and desire to help others and brought about the capacity to truly love.

God wants us to be free of evil and to live with Him for all eternity in righteousness and love. He gives us every tool to do so. God's love for us is so great that He sent His Son to give His life so we could be saved from the captivity of the sin which dooms us to the Lake of Fire. He has given us the gift of scripture to help us learn. He wants all men to be saved and He wants us to succeed. The miracle is that as we reach out to help others, our own pain, our sadness and our anger diminishes, and God places peace and joy in our hearts.

NOTES

Photography by Leon Meyer

Manenberg, Western Cape, South Africa

Chapter Six

THE DESIRE TO OVERCOME

Most of us view some sins as inconsequential and other sins as heinous. We feel that overcoming little sins is an easy task if we put our mind to it, while the larger sins may be more difficult to overcome. But few of us view sin, especially the "little" sins as a captivity with which a spirit of this world can imprison us, keep us from God, and further impel us to repeat our sins. Few of us understand that the white garment we must wear to the wedding feast following the First Resurrection represents the total absence of sin and does not excuse even the smallest stain of the smallest sin.

Scripture tells us in Romans 5:12 *"Wherefore.....for that all have sinned."* And 1 Timothy 2:2-4 tells us *"....that we may lead a quiet and peaceable life in all godliness and honesty. For this is good and acceptable in the sight of God our Savior; Who will have all men to be saved, and to come to the knowledge of the truth."* Through these verses we understand that not one among us is without sin and that each of us must individually find our way to Christ to obtain the forgiveness we require. We also learn that it is through the truth of God's words that we can find what we seek, and in full and true remorse for our sins, find forgiveness. Ephesians 4:14-15, explains, *"That we henceforth be no more children, tossed to and fro, and carried about with every wind of doctrine, by the sleight of men, and cunning craftiness, where they lie in wait to deceive. But speaking the truth in love, may grow up into him in all things, which is the head, even Christ."*

These words show us that God is aware of our status as children who make mistakes, but also shows us that God expects us to mature and put aside those inclinations by learning what He asks of us, and placing His words into our hearts and actions. 1 John 3:8 clearly says, *"He that committeth sin is of the devil; for the devil commiteth sin from the beginning. For this purpose the Son of God was manifested, that he might destroy the works of the devil."* 11 Corinthians 5:17, explains, *"Therefore if any man be in Christ, he is a new creature; old things are passed away; behold, all things are become new."* 11 Corinthians 5: 21 instructs, "*For he hath made him to be sin for us, who knew no sin; that we might be made the righteousness of God in him."* Romans 5:20-21, tells us, *".....where sin abounded, grace did much more abound; That as sin hath reigned unto death, even so might grace reign through righteousness unto eternal life by Jesus Christ our Lord."*

Without the sacrifice of Christ all men would be bound forever with Satan in the second death of eternal torment and none would have eternal life with God. Through Christ however, grace has been offered to those who will follow Christ through both their belief **and the works which that belief inspires**. Throughout scripture the requirement to learn of God's words is tantamount. Without knowing these words we cannot know God and without that knowledge we cannot please God. **It is not just a matter of faith, but a "doing and working" which our faith requires and which creates in our hearts the strength and desire to grow into the Bride of Christ.**

John 14:21 explains, "*He that hath my commandments, and keepeth them, he it is that loveth me....and I will love him, and manifest myself to him.....*" John 14:23-24 tells us, "*....if a man love me, he will keep my words, and we will come unto him, and make our abode with him. He that loveth me not keepeth not my sayings; and the word* *which ye hear is not mine.....”* John 14:26 says, *“But the Comforter, which is the Holy Ghost, whom the Father will send in my name, he shall teach you in all things, and bring all things to your remembrance, whatsoever I have said unto you.”* James 2:17 emphatically states that *“Even so **faith, if it hath not works, is dead,** being alone.”* James 2:26 tells us, *“For as the body without the spirit is dead, so **faith without works is dead** also.”*

It follows that if works must accompany our faith we cannot *know* what works we need to do without knowing God’s instructions about *how* we should work. **Works of faith include how we should treat one another, how we should instruct, exhort, rebuke ourselves, our family, and our neighbors and how we can utilize the sacraments God provides.** We learn that these works include prayer, tithing, keeping the Sabbath holy, listening to and learning the word of God and fully understanding and utilizing the sacraments. We must understand evil, why we are stalked, how to fend off temptation, and become teachers of all these things.

All sin is unacceptable to God. If we acknowledge this and seek forgiveness for every sin, we please God. When we study His word and become enlightened by the incredible scope of what true love shows us, we become more aware of what sin is and how we can changes our lives. What was once a sin of no consequence soon becomes a sin of great consequence because we have been enlightened by the love we learn through knowing God.

We are born with the ability to love **but only selfishly**, whereby we seek only personal reward. But **as we bask under the perfect love of Our Heavenly Father and His Son and their willingness to forgive us, we begin to see love in an unselfish light** and learn how to serve others and appreciate their service. When we experience the perfect love which Christ and our Heavenly Father so freely give us, we cannot help but want to emulate that love by doing what is pleasing to them. A miracle of transformation occurs as we shed the selfish love of our Adam-like nature for the perfect love of the Christ-like nature.

God has provided us with the promise that if we sincerely strive to learn and do what He asks, He will reward us immensely and forgive our mistakes. In Matthew 25:21 God says, *".....Well done, thou good and faithful servant: thou hast been faithful over a few things, I will make thee ruler over many things: enter thou into the joy of thy lord."*

Scripture tells us that God refers to us as His children, and also tells us that He wants us to become the bride of Christ. These descriptions present an expectation of an expanding maturity as we grow from child to bride. Scripture further supports this expectation of development in 1 Corinthians 13:11 where we are told, *"When I was a child, I spake as a child, I understood as a child, I thought as a child, but when I became a man, I put away childish things."*

The blood of the Lamb is the sacrifice which Christ made so our sins could be forgiven. The word "washing" is indicative of two processes which go hand in hand. The first requires the act of acknowledging one's sins, feeling remorse for having committed them, striving to overcome the tendency to commit them again, and succeeding in much of that striving. The second part of the process is accepting and partaking of the sacrament of Holy Communion provided by the sacrifice of Christ. This is the actual washing or cleansing of our sins which can take place worthily only through the actions mentioned above. Perfection cannot be attained while we are in the flesh and living in Satan's territory.

But God rewards us for our contrition, our diligent striving to apply His words to our lives, and for our thankfulness for the forgiveness of sin. In time, these help develop us into the overcomer who has grown in faith and made changes, whereby **our former ways and former temptations have been laid aside and we work toward behavior which is godly.** As mentioned in an earlier chapter, without honest introspection Satan can blind us to our sins and fill us with self-importance, arrogance and pride.

God tells us in Romans 12:2, *"Be not conformed to this world; but be ye transformed by the renewing of your mind, that ye may prove what is that good and acceptable and perfect will of God."* We are also told that we must be careful not to become entangled in evil. Galatians 5:1 warns, *"Be ye not entangled again with the yoke of bondage."* This indicates that **it is possible for us to become entangled *again* even after we break away from sin and even after God himself frees us.**

Thus, to be an overcomer, we need to protect ourselves from the traps which might once again engage us, and even in this God, aware of our fragility, offers us protection. Ephesians 6:11 clearly says, *"Put on the whole armour of God, that ye may be able to stand against the wiles of the devil."* This tells us that without the armour God provides we may not be able to stand against evil.

Further, Romans 13:12 teaches, *"The night is far spent, the day is at hand; let us therefore cast off the works of darkness and let us put on the armour of light."* Here we are told that it is imperative to denounce all former errors, begin making changes in our life, and obtain this armour quickly. We are warned that there is not much time left before Christ returns and that when He does return, it will be too late. The armour itself is righteousness. However, righteousness cannot be obtained without faith. **Faith comes from our relationship with God. And that relationship is developed by learning of God, knowing what He asks of us, striving to do what He asks, developing a close relationship with Him and having our sins forgiven.**

The word “darkness” is indicative of all things evil and the word “light” represents Christ and all He taught and all He sacrificed for us. To obtain the armour or protection of God, we must denounce all things which are the works of darkness and embrace all things which Christ brought us. When we have done our best toward this goal, God will empower us to withstand evil even when it is at its peak of strength. If we have done our due diligence and we have obtained the armour God offers, He promises that we will withstand the evil at the end of days.

The end of days or the “end times” as described in scripture clearly tells us that even the children of God will suffer great tribulation. Scripture explains that it will be our faith and our trust in God which will help us through those days until Christ returns. It explains that **as Christians are persecuted and evil appears to prosper and God does not stop that evil, many will question their faith and even**

lose it. This is a clear warning about what we will face during the end times.

The problem facing those who have not had the time to build that trust is that what they have built may be too fragile to stand. This is why it is so important to begin to develop and test our trust so we can stand strong in those days of evil. Thus **God allows us to face our trials and tribulations *now* so we will not fail later.**

One part of depression is that it robs us of the trust we must have that God will care for us and bring us through every circumstance. Therefore learning how to overcome depression is important. Satan brings the sadness and exhaustion into our lives in the hope that we will no longer expect God to help. Such a lack of expectation and trust pushes us away from a close relationship with God. However, prayer, recalling the scripture which teaches us of God's love for us, and His promises to us, and saying no to negative thoughts help us fight off the lack of expectation that our circumstances will change and that we will emerge from our battle victorious and better for it.

God will always create a blessing from our heartache if we trust Him. He tells us that He knows how many hairs are on our head thus knows every thought and struggle we have. He reminds us in scripture that if He cares for the birds in winter why wouldn't He care for His children. When the difficult waters of life edge up from our ankles to our chest and climb to our neck and we raise our chin we will not drown. When the waters continue to move from our neck over our lips we tilt our head and breathe through our nostrils, knowing that the waters will never cover our nose. And it doesn't because God will not allow it. As we trust God when the waters rise, the power we draw increases and the waters ***must*** recede. God will always lead us to what or who can help us overcome if we trust Him and allow Him to work in our lives.

Scripture clearly warns that many will not be found worthy and tells us that as guardians of His words, we must enlighten others by preaching, teaching, exhorting, and rebuking so that all can learn. It is not too late to be forgiven or to turn our lack of knowledge into enlightenment or to turn a hardened heart into a loving and contrite and humble heart. It is not too late for us to win the battle Satan has launched against us and overcome

NOTES

Photography by Matthew Burniston
City of Bradford, West Yorkshire, England

Chapter Seven

STRUGGLES AND FAILURES

We live in a busy world filled with tension, anxiety, envy, and perceived wrongs. These breed a strong anger which many release on the nearest, least dangerous object. Often someone's anger is surprising because we saw no need for it and no manner in which it served to solve a problem. However, most of us feel anger from time to time and many of us feel guilty about the ease and immediacy with which our anger surfaces. Sometimes it is the little things which add up and cause our anger, but more often it is something sudden which surprises us and is the initial reaction to real or perceived pain, loss, rejection, fear or tension.

Today's world is filled with anger because so many have lost the peace which knowing and trusting God can create in our hearts. Road rage is one such example. Naturally, we should feel righteous anger in certain situations, and even express that anger in some cases. But it is the control, the letting go, and the action of that anger with which we need concern ourselves. Anger is natural, but the hate or harm and the judgment which stems from anger are satanic. As we grow, we mature and we presumably learn self control. But Satan employs every possible avenue to produce anger and uses it to reach his goal of creating disharmony and causing isolation.

While self control does not mean that we cannot feel anger, it does mean that we must express that anger in a limited fashion. As we learn what God tells us about expressing anger, we learn how to counteract its negative influence with something positive. God can open our understanding of temporal things, but we must be willing to learn and apply the spiritual aspect to our use of and reaction to our anger to find a permanent solution to our problems.

In today's world, anxiety is a part of everyone's life, but it's the control of that anxiety which will limit our anger and fear, and comes from trusting God with our life. Overcoming is enhanced when we understand our psyche or our natural inclinations, as well. The study of psychology teaches that anxiety attacks are from continuous tension which occasionally explodes into intense panic and can cause irreparable harm, thus its progression needs to be limited. Anxiety or panic attacks can last a few minutes or a few hours. Sweating, apprehension, a pounding heart, or a feeling that you have lost control, can't breathe, are having a heart attack, or are fearful of dying are all symptoms. These can be very frightening.

Also, conversion reaction can occur where anxiety is converted into more severe physical symptom resembling disease or disability. This is another symptom of anxiety which can encourage the quick response of anger because of the fear and concern it can produce in both the one who is depressed and those around them.

We "learn" to react to anxiety and in fact, any threat, but can unlearn that reaction if the old causal conditions are removed. **God can help us "unlearn" reactions by removing our fear and increasing our trust through the safety of our relationship with Him.** Sadly we can also carry anger which we have suppressed for a long time, and transfer it to the only acceptable emotion we are "allowed" to have, which is depression. Studies indicate that the act of reconciliation often dissipates anger and depression, but the question which plagues the child of God is "how does one reconcile if the same harmful acts are committed over and over again?"

Matthew 5:25 says, "*Leave there thy gift before the altar, and go thy way; first be reconciled to thy brother, and then come and offer thy gift*" but how is this done when someone does not have remorse for the harm they cause and will behave in the same manner again and again? Can one of two parties reconcile?

If someone ***does*** ask for forgiveness it is much easier for us to forgive. If we love the soul yet are "allowed" to openly hate the actions, we can be honest about our feelings and work toward resolving the negatives our feelings create. But when we bury what has occurred, allow it to fester for a long period of time, there is a lingering infection. This occurs when there is a lack of remorse on the part of those who brought us harm.

Thus, there was and is no closure in the *natural* sense to what occurred. While we understand that Satan is the real cause of all hurtful behavior, we face a dilemma because if we *excuse* someone's actions based on our belief that Satan directed that person, we can easily feel that we have compromised our principles by not speaking against that action. Additionally, excusing inappropriate behavior causes us to transfer the anger or the fear we experience from that behavior to someone else, possibly even to ourselves.

For example, those who are afraid to confront an abuser will often blame the abused because it is safer to transfer anger to someone who would not respond to their anger by causing them harm. Thus a father's abuse is often blamed on the mother, which is a classic case of transference and occurs quite often in families. The directive here is to acknowledge the problem, assess it accurately for what it is, openly place the anger where it belongs, condemn the sin, and ***don't stay where the sin can***

continue to occur....yet be willing to forgive the soul for sinning. That way there's no baggage to carry.

God often gets angry when we consciously sin. He forgives us when we repent, but is angry again when He sees us continue in those sins, especially when we know better. Yet **He always forgives us when He sees that we are repentant and that we want to overcome these tendencies.** Through scripture, God warns us to run (flee) from sin and this means from the sin of other's as well as our own.

We can lay aside anger if we understand anger, and understand that it is often misdirected. If we don't understand its protective or reactive components, nor recognize our personal shortcomings, we can't acknowledge or overcome them. If we don't seek the right relationship with God where He can direct us to the truth, teach us about evil and rebuking the spirits which seek to harm us, we find it difficult to change. Nor can we heal from the harm others have done to us if we don't acknowledge their actions as sin inspired by evil and, if it occurs repeatedly, to leave. Once we leave, we can work on letting our anger go.

If that person seeks us again, we can rebuke their sin, admonish them and forgive, but *not remain for further abuse.* If we don't take these steps, then the problem will always be lurking in our lives and also in our subconscious waiting to resurface again, waiting to cause us anger and anxiety, and pushing us toward living in an ungodly atmosphere.

The Bible tells us *how* we are to handle the sin of others. Christ always acknowledged sin when he saw it and He was angered by it. **Often we sweep sin under the table and enable it to flourish by not rebuking it.** But Christ utilized God's protection and the angel service to keep His anger in a Godly perspective. He never used his anger to bring harm to anyone. He prayed, He testified, He rebuked, and then He forgave but He often gave the admonishment to "Go and sin no more".

Evil spirits can cause a person to be cruel and Christ recognized those spirits in those with whom He interacted. When Christ called a spirit by name, acknowledging it and rebuking it, the spirit could no longer hide, thus when Christ demanded the spirit leave, it did. The Bible describes this in Mark 9:25 where it says, *When Jesus saw that the people came running together, he rebuked the foul spirit, saying unto him, Thou dumb and deaf spirit, I charge thee, come out of him, and enter no more into him.*

Perhaps we cannot make a spirit leave someone, but we can call it out so it knows we see it, and we can then rebuke it. Further, we can pray that the hold the spirit has will be weakened. Scripture and psychology books both reinforce similar conclusions for dealing with the pain others bring to us. Words like projection, rationalization, transference, displacement, suppression, and denial and what the reactions they describe are similar to much of what is described in scripture in the attitude of the Pharisees, the accusations of those who persecuted Christ, and the actions of Judas.

For example, projection occurs when someone transfers one's own shortcoming onto someone else. Many abusers and alcoholics blame everyone but themselves for what they do. They choose a scapegoat for their displaced aggression and project their own shortcomings on that target, denying they are taking their aggression out on an innocent person. **If they were not in denial, the abuser would have to see himself as a coward. He rationalizes his behavior, offering excuses, blaming others, and feeling justified in his cruel acts**. He suppresses and consciously puts his actions out of his mind. He is too cowardly to deal with his problems.

The word "anger" in the concordance shows us many verses throughout the Bible which indicates

God's anger. In Exodus 32:22 Aaron said, "*....Let not the anger of my Lord wax hot . . .*" In Numbers 11:10 scriptures tells us, "*.....and the anger of the Lord was kindled greatly . . .*" And in Deuteronomy 4: 25 we are told, "*....and shall do evil in the sight of the Lord thy God, to provoke him to anger;....*"

Further, it is interesting to note that scripture also tells us that God is sometimes comforted by His anger. Ezekiel 5: 13 says: "*Thus shall mine anger be accomplished, and I will cause my fury to rest upon them, and I will be comforted . . .*" However, God has the right to judge, punish, and be angry at both the soul and the deed because He is without sin. We, on the other hand, have sinned and have no right to judge others. We cannot be angry with the soul, but *can* and should be angry at the deed. A limited expression of anger toward the deed is a rebuke against evil. This is important to understand because if the Bible tells us we *can* express anger at the sin and acknowledge the sin, and this admonition agrees with the psychology books which say that when we suppress anger it can be detrimental to our personal well being, we can rest in the fact that expressing anger even if only at the deed itself is important for avoiding what could harm us both spiritually and physically.

God brought the wrath of His anger to those with whom he was angry, but *we* can't do this because it is not our right. Even God holds back His full anger. Jeremiah 30:24 tells us that God is holding back His anger now: *"The fierce anger of the Lord shall not return, until he have done it, and until he have performed the intents of his heart: in the latter days ye shall consider it."*

Through this verse we know that not only is God holding back, planning the right time to vent his anger for the evil which has been done, but also that this "right time" will be the latter days, the end times which we have now entered. Genesis 6:6 says "*....and it grieved him at his heart*" and Genesis

8:21 says, "*...behold I will destroy them with the earth*" and in Genesis 9:15, "*...And the waters shall no more become a flood to destroy all flesh*". The story of the flood teaches us that God was so angered by the sinfulness he found on earth that He sent the flood to destroy the perpetration of sin by destroying the sinners. But after they were destroyed, God felt grieved and didn't want to express His anger in destruction again until the very end days. God sent the rainbow to mark the covenant He then made with man not to destroy unrepentant sinners again *until* the bride of Christ is removed from the earth.

The New Testament also addresses anger. The words of Christ in Mark 3:5 tell us, *"And when he had looked round about on them with anger, being grieved for the hardness of their hearts, he saith . . ."* Christ was perfect. He did not sin. He went to the cross completely unblemished, free from sin. Therefore when the Bible shows us that Christ was angry, it also shows us that *justified* anger, correctly *checked* and understood, is acceptable. Yet Christ endured terrible grief. He was subjected to disloyalty, disbelief, and outright hatred. Isaiah 53:3 tells us, *"He is despised and rejected of men; a man of sorrows, and acquainted with grief:..."* And Proverbs 29:27 tells us, *"An unjust man is an abomination to the just: and he that is upright in the way is abomination to the wicked"*.

As believers in Christ, we are also hated by many. We are forewarned that we have enemies in this world and that **those who are wicked will seek to harm us.** The wicked are ruled and inspired by Satan and we must walk in God's words so we can obtain His protection and direction and we must not respond with hatred. We must trust that God will avenge the harm others bring us. Romans 12:19 tells us, *"Dearly beloved, avenge not yourselves, but rather give place unto wrath; for it is written, Vengeance is mine; I will repay, saith the Lord."*

NOTES

Photography by Matthew Burniston
City of Bradford, West Yorkshire, England

Chapter Eight

THE BEGINNING OF CHANGE

Much of what some term "Christian Guilt" stems from the acknowledgement that we do not and cannot always live up to the very principles we espouse. We simply cannot be perfect in the practice of all the aspirations set before us as children of God no matter how hard we try. And, we often commiserate over our failures even when we repent our mistakes and strive to do better in the future. Yet it is our failures which keep us humble, remind us of how much we need God, and how blessed we are to have been brought into our faith.

Our failures also impel us to appreciate the unconditional love so evident in the sacrifice God made for us when He provided us with the forgiveness of sin. God tells us that when we have sinned and we have repented with remorse and the hope that we will not repeat that same sin, and have received Holy Communion worthily, He remembers that sin no more. In other words, our sin is forgotten.

Hebrews 8:12 tells us, *"For I will be merciful to their unrighteousness, and their sins and their iniquities will I remember no more."* Hebrews 10:14, 17 also tell us, *"For by one offering he hath perfected for ever them that are sanctified. And their sins and iniquities will I remember no more."*

Sometimes however, and as mentioned in a previous chapter, situations arise which require us to remember what occurred in order to protect ourselves and others from future harm. While forgetting past indiscretions helps us move on and helps us find the peace we need in our lives, sometimes, as in all good things, we expand one good point into 'rules' which bring more harm than good. We misunderstand the proper meaning and context of the original thought. We increase our anxieties by an unnecessary ideology which we find difficult to fulfill.

God gave us our memories for a reason. When we remember, for instance, how badly it hurt when we touched a hot stove, we are careful not to touch a hot stove again. **We use our memories to keep us from those things which may bring us harm, and to draw to us those things which bring us joy.** Our memories also enhance our faith and help us make the tough choices when we must act out of our faith. Faith is actually the *memory* of (trust in) what God has done for us. Hebrews 11: 7, 8 reminds us, "*By faith Noah, being warned of God of* *things not seen as yet, moved with fear, prepared an ark to the saving of his house; by the which he condemned the world, and became heir of the righteousness which is by faith. By faith Abraham, when he was called to go out into a place which he should after receive for an inheritance, obeyed and went out, not knowing whither he went."*

This tells us that faith brings us the strength to act as God asks rather than as our inclinations might momentarily suggest. When someone acts not as God has asked and harms one of His children, He remembers those acts and, if they do not repent, tells us that *He* will take vengeance.

In fact, the only time God forgets is when those He loves and who love Him make mistakes, truly repent, and ask for forgiveness. Then he gladly forgets their sins and remembers them no longer. God remembers the remorse He felt after he'd sent the flood and is thus slow to act and longsuffering in the hope that those who sin will eventually have regrets.

However, for the child of God, misplaced guilt and some erroneous teachings demand that when we forgive someone we are to also forget what was done to harm us **despite the fact that there is no scripture to support this statement. In fact, t**here is **danger** in practicing this misconception. God wants us to have peace and joy in our lives. He also wants us to be armed at all times to fight the wickedness we face which is inspired by Satan. To have peace, we cannot carry guilt, especially when that guilt is misplaced and we must remember what can bring us harm.

Remembering danger is a protective measure and a healthy practice as long as we have forgiven the soul for committing that deed. The keywords here are, 'if we have forgiven them.' God wants us to forgive, but He has ***not*** asked us to forget. When God tells us to arm ourselves so we can fight the spiritual wickedness which seeks to devour us, the armour He speaks of is His words, His instruction, and His protection. When our heart is right with God and we continue to seek to learn and do what He asks of us, His direction and protection is ours. He protects us from dangers, but warns us that **we have a responsibility to be prudent,** to be aware of evil, to seek to be equally yoked, and **to 'watch' for evil.... and flee it. We cannot watch for what is forgotten.**

1 Peter 4:7 tells us, *"But the end of all things is at hand; be ye therefore sober, and watch unto prayer."* 1 Peter 5:8 says, *"Be sober, be vigilant, because your adversary the devil, as a roaring lion, walketh about, seeking who he may devour."*

False prophets will come and we must watch for their errors so we do not fall prey to their teachings. Evil circles us and tempts us and we must remember their end, so we are not tempted. Even family members may denounce God. We are told in

Matthew 10:21, *"....children shall rise up against their parents and cause them to be put to death."*

Thus, as mentioned previously, **we must remember just as we must forgive. We must be watchful and careful just as we are forgiving and loving.** We must not let our guard down as these end times are fulfilled, for God clearly warns in Mark 13:20, *"And except that the Lord hath shortened, those days, no flesh should be saved; but for the elect's sake, whom he hath chosen, he hath shortened them."* Once we begin to value self and seek to protect ourselves as God teaches, and to trust God, we know that we have begun to change.

While it is difficult to live through heartbreaking circumstances especially when thoughts come that God does not hear nor answer our prayers, we suddenly realize that we are now approaching these circumstances with less fear. This is an indicator of how we have changed. When difficulties continued in the past with no end in sight we may have become discouraged and perhaps questioned our faith, or questioned our worthiness to have our prayers heard. We may have even wondered what we did wrong to deserve what had befallen us. Now we understand that these are the **normal** reactions of our Adam-like nature, but they are not godly; they come from Satan and must be fought….. and that our trust in God helps us fight them.

Satan wants us discouraged by heartache and wants us to blame God, feel unworthy of His help, and question His lack of intervention. We learn through scripture that when Satan succeeded in causing Adam and Eve to sin and thereby opened the door to sin, we were subject to battle not only our own sin, but the inherited sin which scripture defines as a type of "generational" sin which is visited upon the third and fourth generations.

This tells us that **the weaknesses of our forefathers may have transferred to us and may be the source of addictions and certain other**

tendencies, which can be difficult to fight. But, God factored this into His plan of salvation and provided us with a way to overcome and He offers His comforting presence and direction during our struggle to do so. Our Heavenly Father, omnipotent and omnipresent, clearly tells us in Romans 8:28, *"And we know that all things work together for good to them that love God, to them who are called according to his purpose."*

There is a reason why we must live through heartache. When we understand why God allows our struggles they are easier to bear and the blessing we can derive from the experience may become evident more quickly. Our job is to believe that a blessing does come from our experience. And to believe that **good comes from what transpires in our heart as we go through our difficult circumstances.**

When we learn what scripture tells us about this phenomenon we can place our faith in God's help and wisdom. Scripture tells us that God does not bring our heartache, but that Satan does, and that God in His perfect righteousness must allow it but will not only bring us through it, but also create of blessing from it .

However, just as God went with Shadrach, Meshach and Abed-nego into the furnace (Daniel 3:20), and with Daniel into the den of lions (Daniel 6:6), and with David when he faced Goliath (1 Samuel 17:49), He goes with us.

God turns our heartache into a blessing in a way that we do not understand but which we later learn has established our loyalty to God and strengthens us in the process.

But when we are not aware that it is Satan who brings our heartache and God creates a blessing from it, our heartache is more difficult to bear, the blessing harder to recognize and the lesson less quickly learned.

The Biblical account of Sodom and Gomorra teaches us God's compassion as we read that He agreed to Abraham's plea (Genesis 18:32) to save Lot and his family from the destruction of the city. We learn of His patience when Jonah ran from God (Jonah 1:3), we understand His gentleness through the beatitudes Christ spoke (Matthew 5:3-11), we see his longsuffering in all His references to us as children rather than adults, and we see His love throughout the beauty of the creation which He designed just for us.

When we have an intimate relationship with our Heavenly Father, His words touch a chord in our heart which allows us to internalize His loving, gentle nature. With these facts in our heart and mind we trust God more easily and are more likely to muster our strength to wait patiently for our circumstances to change or to follow the directives He has placed in front of us. We can dismiss our fear, anxiety, and doubt, and most importantly, thank God for our circumstances because we know that they bring valuable changes to our heart to create in us one who can become a part of the Bride of Christ.

Fellowship with other true believers can help us. If we share our worries and triumphs with one another and bear one another's burdens we will uplift one another in times of sorrow. We can pray for one another, remind one another of the various verses in scripture which may pertain to our circumstance, bask in the promise that God never leaves us, and love, forgive and encourage one another. We also share how much God loves us as we relate our miracles of faith and how God teaches us through the difficulties Satan brings into our lives.

God works miracles through what we go through and is pleased when we use our experiences to help others move through their difficulties. He wants us to grow from children of God into the Bride of Christ which can only be accomplished if we develop in love and understanding, compassion and strength.

As is often said, if we never felt pain, we would not know that God is our healer. If we never had to pray we would not know that He delivers us from our difficulties. If we never felt sadness, we would not feel His comfort. If we never had a trial to go through, we could never call ourselves overcomers. If we were never in trouble, how would we know that God always comes to our rescue? If we never suffered, how would we understand the suffering of others, or what Christ suffered on the cross? And if we were never broken, how would we learn that God can make us whole? If our life was perfect, we might not have the opportunity to know God and recognize how much we need Him and how much He does for us.

We should marvel at how profound it is that God turns evil into good so that all things work for the good of those who love the Lord. And, we should marvel at how much this can comfort us as we go through our trials and tribulations.

We also have the incredible promise of Revelation 2:10: *"Fear none of those things which thou shalt suffer...."* When we can fully believe these words, we will not be dismayed by the circumstances which some our way.

And Revelation 21:4: *"And God shall wipe away all tears from their eyes; and there shall be no more death, neither sorrow, nor crying, neither shall there be any more pain...."*

NOTES

Photography by Janet Reed Lourens

Johannesburg, South Africa

Chapter Nine

SUCCESS HAS ITS OWN STRUGGLES

Healing is a process whereby we become more aware of our circumstances and how we have responded to them. As we heal and begin to identify the causes and necessary changes required, we can become angry at ourselves and at those who may have caused our pain. Acknowledging our feelings can be cathartic, but expressing it in a negative manner can be harmful. As mentioned earlier, everyone, good or bad, gets angry. God even gets angry. Christ too, once became so angry that He overturned the market tables inside the gates of the temple. There are differences however between feeling anger, expressing anger, and maintaining anger. **How we handle our anger is a mark of our character.** Anger is a natural consequence of the Adam-like nature but as we move from the Adam-like nature to the Christ-like nature we learn…and desire… to control our anger.

Many emotions can produce anger because we don't always know how to handle those emotions. We can express anger, but not always express jealousy or envy, fear or anxiety or any other emotion which is uncomfortable. Feeling anger however, often moves into expressing anger and this comes in two forms; one is productive and the other negative.

Productive expression is when we calmly acknowledge, and explain, that we felt anger over a certain situation, why we felt that anger, and what we believe should be put into place to prevent the cause of that anger in the future. This helps us avoid circumstances which cause anger and helps us explain to others what upsets us and how to avoid it.

Negative expression occurs when we openly express our feelings in a manner which angers others and we offer no constructive explanation of, or methods for, preventing the cause of our anger. A negative reaction demonstrates that we have not controlled our anger, have not directed it toward solutions based in love and respect, and that we do not actively seek resolution. This is detrimental to those around us and detrimental to our soul salvation.

The act of maintaining our anger is encouraged by Satan and must be overcome. While the memory of what caused our anger may serve to keep us from harm, the maintenance or harboring of anger works to cloud our judgment, prevent change and growth, and robs us of love. It also removes our ability to maintain the fruits of the Holy Spirit which strives to guide us toward perfect love. Harboring anger can also make us ill because it destroys our peace, and creates anxiety, hate and other detrimental emotions. It also means that we have not forgiven.

Forgiving others is necessary to obtaining our own forgiveness through Holy Communion. Our worthiness when taking Holy Communion is dependent upon either our forgiving others or **sincerely *striving* to forgive** others for the harm they caused. When Christ was asked what the most important commandment was, he said that we should love God with all our being and love our neighbor as ourselves.

God has granted grace to us *on the condition* that we take the sacrament of Holy Communion *worthily.* God understands that sometimes we continue to feel the hurt caused by someone or some deed. He therefore graciously accepts our *honest* efforts to work toward forgiveness knowing that this effort may not produce results overnight but will eventually.

We can promote forgiveness in our heart through the powerful tool of prayer asking God to help us forgive, and asking for the peace that Christ said He gladly gives us. We cannot condemn and judge the person who brought us harm because God has stated that He will take vengeance *for* us and that *our* job is to forgive. **Our worthiness depends on us doing so.**

Furthermore, we don't know what conditions exist in the person who brought us harm. They may not yet know God, they may be pawns in Satan's hands; they may have suffered abuse themselves, they may labor under the captivity of jealousy from which they cannot escape. Or, we may have misinterpreted what they said or did. Thus God asks us to wait, to trust that He will handle their indiscretions, and asks that we forgive so ***we* are not burdened by *their* faults** and failings.

God also tells us that **He will bless us** for striving to behave in this manner. It is up to the other person then to seek their own forgiveness from God, from those they harmed, and to make restitution for the harm they caused. If they don't seek forgiveness or try to make restitution, God will deal with them.

Christ brought His message in love and gentleness and then allowed His message to take root as men took that message home with them. We too can bring a message, but it must not be presented in a manner which will evoke anger. Scripture explains that in time the power of love and prayer, and of our personal example, can *cause* our message to take root. Psalm 133:1 tells us, *"Behold, how good and how pleasant it is for brethren to dwell together in unity!"*

Being angry with someone who caused our suffering, when God offers us a blessing for handling it correctly, makes no sense. We receive something incredibly valuable by handling our anger correctly. Satan may inspire someone to hurt us, but God can turn it into a blessing for us. **This is one of the most magnificent miracles of our life of faith and those who harm us have no idea of the gift that the harm they brought us can actually provide for us!** If we learn how this process works, we can overcome a great deal. We can help ourselves and we can help others. We can stand firm when we are attacked knowing that God loves us and will create a miracle from our experience. Even if we fall prey to fear or anger temporarily, we can work out of it, rise above it, and bring joy to the heart of God in the process.

Colossians 3:21 tells us: *"Fathers, provoke not your children to anger, lest they be discouraged."* Hebrews 13:6 tells us: *"So that we may boldly say, The Lord is my helper, and I will not fear what man shall do unto me"*. Hebrews 13:16 tells us: *"But to do good and to communicate forget not; for with such sacrifices God is well pleased."*

Matthew 7:12 tells us: *"Therefore all things whatsoever ye would that men should do to you, do ye even so to them...."* And Proverbs 16:24 tells us: *"Pleasant words are as a honeycomb; sweet to the soul, and health to the bones."* Proverbs 8:32 tells us: *"....for blessed are they that keep my ways."*

Anger has its place and sometimes we must be angry. But in most cases we become angry over something that doesn't really matter. Scripture teaches us that **the bottom line is to rebuke evil, and flee from evil,** but love the soul, and where possible, keep peace with one another. The true children of God must work together to learn and teach God's words to be a part of the First Resurrection, and must overcome the traps Satan brings. .

However, some people are governed by evil and they are best left to God to handle. Some are so arrogant that they would never consider that what they do is wrong. But we must consider that there is the possibility that if we refuse to forgive someone and retain our anger toward them, it could be that God has answered *their* pleas for forgiveness and **they will have *our* place** at the wedding feast because of our inability to forgive. What is imperative is that we overcome the tendency to make a blanket judgment of what others do.

Scripture teaches us to love one another, care for one another, and forgive one another, but not to judge one another….that is up to God alone. Our job is to continually examine with honesty whether or not **we** are doing what God asks of us. We are to let our anger go and to forgive all harm even if we must remember it to protect ourselves in the future.

While we might be better served to avoid interaction with those who are governed by evil, God asks that we always forgive the soul because only He… not we… know what causes that soul to sin. If we strive to do as He asks, He promises to look after everything else.

Nevertheless, when faced with those who remain arrogant and selfish, judgmental and filled with pride, envy or hate, there is no harm in separating politely and with kindness to maintain one's peace. However, any separation such as this does require that we pray for those who we may deem our enemy or who we think may bring us harm. Even if we must flee from the sprits they entertain, because God asks that we love all souls, we must do our part even if it is behind the scenes by praying for them.

What this does for our soul is to free it from any guilt or remorse and to create in it the Christ-like nature God longs for us to develop. Loving one another requires that we recognize, and accept with certain parameters, their shortcomings, and appreciate their strengths. To understand why we are all so different and why God is so willing to provide every opportunity to every sinner is beautifully explained by what we see in a garden.

If we were to imagine ourselves walking in a large and beautiful garden filled with every plant ever created we would find incredible diversity. There would be those which appear to have been created for their beauty, some short lived and others long lasting, some for their strength against the elements and others for their aroma. Some were created for their medicinal value and some claim such a dense growth that they stifle all weeds, others offer us a cascading grace which reaches far from their roots. One is not necessarily better than another. Each can claim their place in the garden and each can proclaim their value.

Interestingly, though God created all these flowers, once sin was introduced into the creation, some no longer work well together. One may tend to crowd out the other, rob its sun, steal its water; another may require an alkaline soil to thrive and another demands an acid soil. Some are poisonous and others are medicinal. Yet God made all these flowers and plants and has made provision for all of them to thrive.... or to wither and die.

People are much the same. We were perfect until sin entered our lives. We lived in harmony until sin caused disharmony. God has created us with black hair, brown hair and blonde hair, He has created us with brown skin and black skin, white skin and yellow skin. He has created people who are tall and short, stocky and thin, with brown eyes and amber eyes, blue eyes or hazel eyes. Some talk a lot, others talk very little, some are strong and others weak, but all of us have hopes, dreams, thoughts and feelings and each of us has been given a talent which we are to nurture and use in service to God.

These differences can make us proud, angry or satisfied or to feel superior or inferior to others. God wants us to appreciate what we have and what we are rather than envy those who we think may have been given more or better. Appreciation for what we have rather than what we want is an important aspect of being content. Because God never makes a mistake, each of us has been perfectly created, perfectly planted, perfectly nourished and placed in our most beneficial environment where we choose to grow or to wither.

Free will allows us to decide which attitude we will embrace. Free will allows us to decide to be thankful or to be angry. Free will forces us to take responsibility for our choices and what those choices bring into our lives. However, through prayer, God helps us recognize what is good for us as opposed to what would be harmful, and He encourages us to choose the path of peace and joy rather than anxiety and anger. He shows us how to bloom where we are planted and how to thrive. He teaches us that evil is always angry and cunning, sly and envious, plotting and malicious, jealous and unappreciative.

Evil however, makes us proud and haughty, self-serving and unloving, while righteousness and thankfulness make us happy and honest, open and supportive, appreciative and humble, giving and loving. Righteousness takes away our fear and replaces it with peace and it is only through God, through the forgiveness of sin that we can find righteousness and all the gifts it provides.

Success demands the struggle that becoming righteous in the eyes of God requires of us but it is a struggle which brings great rewards and an incredible future not tied to material possessions, beauty or talent, but tied only to the heart.

"For God shall bring every work

into judgment, with every secret thing

whether it be good, or whether it be evil."

Ecclesiastes 12:14

NOTES

Photography by Peter Herring

Thornton, Western Cape, South Africa

Chapter Ten

PSYCHOLOGICAL OR BIOCHEMICAL?

God also uses people to help people. He can direct our path to those who can help us learn how to help ourselves. He can bless those to whom we turn to for help by giving them godly wisdom. When we seek help, it is best to ask God to direct us to the right people. Learning what the experts say and learning the terminology they might employ allows us to be well informed and helps us make the best decisions. There are a variety of paths one can choose to find help and one may be better suited to our situation than another. Thus "doing our homework" is very beneficial because if those paths remain unknown, we cannot utilize them.

So far, this book has discussed some of the spiritual aspects of developing a close relationship with God and the plan of salvation He has created for us. It has also discussed why we often face heartache and why we need to learn what God tells us through scripture. It has suggested that we also need to speak to and pray with our ministers. But it may also be beneficial to explore our problem with an expert who is well trained to assist us with our problems. If it is a medical problem, we seek a physician, if it is a psychological problem, we may seek the advice of a psychologist or psychiatrist. But whoever we seek, we must first seek God's guidance through prayer and through the blessing we can obtain through our bearers of blessing…our ministers.

When we seek outside help, it is very beneficial to learn some of the terminology related to what we suffer so we can better understand what options we may have and how those who counsel us draw their conclusions about our needs. Discussing our situation with a medical professional helps us learn whether or not we face a problem which requires further exploration and more specified treatment. Learning what may be the cause of our problem and understanding how it can be solved removes any hesitancy we might have about receiving the treatment associated with resolving the issue.

When we explore the world of depression, we find that there are many terms describing why our emotions might run amuck, and learn that there are various approaches for counseling, for treatment, and for medications. We learn that there can be both or singularly biological component and a psychological component which offer many treatment options. Exploring first the biochemical component guides us to the pros and cons of the medications which might be suggested and the alternative to these medications.

All patented chemical medications offer both a benefit and a side effect. Some of the side effects are not beneficial, but can often be managed. However, when medications are suggested, it is helpful to explore and discuss whether or not there is an alternative to those medications. In some cases chemical medications have a nutritional counterpart.

When we have fully explored these routes to healing, we can then ask questions to determine which might work best for us. By doing this, we are participating in the healing process by understanding why we engage a particular remedy and will know all the options we may have for the healing process. Medication and nutrition are but two of these components.

Since our emotions can exercise a tremendous power over our bodies, minds and behavior, we should also examine the psychology related to the symptoms we might manifest. The tenets of psychology explain that emotions are "hypothetical constructs" meaning that they cannot be fully observed because they can be hidden or indescribable. As an example, rage, grief, joy, jealousy, ecstasy, sadness, and boredom are but some of the terms used to describe how we feel.

We cannot measure these and we cannot compare one person's emotion to another except through what is inferred by our actions and reactions or by what someone tells us. Emotions are however, a part of the human state and play an important role in how we handle life and how much we are willing or able to do to get well.

Studies have shown that rage, fear and joy are unlearned and are present at birth. Thus, they are a part of the Adam-like nature which protects a newborn and entices its caregiver into meeting its needs. Even as adults our fears often continue to protect us and our joy often draws friendships and fellowship. Rage however, is or should be taught to be subdued and is generally socially unacceptable.

Some studies conclude that experiencing both fear and joy together produces guilt, and that experiencing affection, joy and fear together produce jealousy. Studies have also indicated that all emotions are present by the age of two years old and that a smile is a universal expression. Most cultures share a similar facial reaction for happiness, pain, fear and sadness. We also similarly express our feelings through body language, which includes our facial expression, our gestures, movements and posture.

Emotional *expression* is the outward or measurable signs of one's feelings. These could be trembling, exhibiting a tense or defensive posture, contorted movement, sweating palms, a pounding heart or other symptoms which can be caused by the release of adrenaline by the nervous system.

Studies have been conducted which indicate that any emotional experience is our own personal *subjective* experience meaning that one person may view or be affected by an experience or event very differently than another. Therefore, the personal intensity which is felt may, in some cause physiological changes which can be detrimental to one's health. Because few of us can discern how severe these reactions may be in someone else, it is important to encourage a professional evaluation if we suspect a problem.

There were three basic studies in the early years of the field of psychology which began the foray into a greater understanding of our psyche. Understanding the sequence of events, and what triggers a response helps us understand how to address the problem.

In 1884-1885 The James-Lange theory was put forth which claimed that bodily changes preceded emotion. This meant that we first experience an action which causes us to want to flee, and this sensation then causes our fear. (Act, determine, interpret)

But then in 1927, The Cannon-Bard Theory was introduced which claimed that the brain determines a danger and immediately issues the fear which then tells us to flee. (Determine, Interpret, act)

In 1964, Schachter's Cognitive Theory of Emotion was introduced which claimed that we had to first label or interpret this experience through past experiences, determine the pros and cons of that experience before we would react. (Interpret, determine, act)

Either way we learn from these theories that according to basic psychology the physical aspects of emotion seem to be built into our bodies. Much of this stems from the "fight or flight" mechanism of the sympathetic nervous system which once activated does not subside for approximately twenty or thirty minutes after a perceived threat has been removed. Some of the observable physical reactions to a perceived threat are dilated pupils, dryness of the eyes, dilated bronchi, increased blood flow, dry throat, elevated blood sugar, cold and clammy skin, increased perspiration and hair standing on end.

Coping with emotion is different from one person to another. The timing of what occurs, the current health and well-being of the person and their recent or past experiences regarding that emotion or occurrence effects how they will react. All of these have their origins in the Adam-like nature which demands the preservation of the species.

Past experiences are very powerful in determining our reaction to events. Learned helplessness is when one resigns themselves to their current fate and it is extremely debilitating. It is when one finally capitulates to passively enduring whatever life has in store for them, rather than actively directing their life in as positive as path as they can. Depression, one of the most widespread emotional problems people now suffer, can move into a learned hopelessness which can impede one from wanting to engage in helping themselves.

Hope is one of the most important components of healing. Studies indicate that learned helplessness can be "unlearned" by a number of successful forays into an emotional danger zone. Thus while subjective feelings, emotional expressions, physiological changes and interpretation of the emotion are the four major parts of an emotion and all play a part in how we feel and act, we can modify their negative components.

The value of hope, which is considered a fragile emotion, is a powerful healing force against depression and helplessness. These determinations coincide with what scripture tells us and support what scripture teaches about the difference between the Adam-like nature of fear and self-preservation, and the Christ-like nature of hope and trust.

If our cognitive appraisal of any threat determines our emotional response, which then produces a fear reaction, we can overcome that response when we trust that God will not allow any harm to come to us despite whatever threat we face.

Scripturally, we know that Satan, aware of the fallibility of the Adam-like nature, uses our negative emotional responses to direct our thinking toward the helpless state. He can then create the circumstances whereby we fall deeper and deeper into a helpless state and become captive to those emotions and thereby captive to him.

The frustration we feel when we try to emerge from that state and fail, creates stress which then creates exhaustion which prevents us from continuing the fight to overcome. Satan then adds the additional stressors of guilt and conflict to further debilitate those he seeks to harm. By awakening family members to the problem but not providing solutions can evoke further anger, rejection, loss, even aggression, and enhance the process of isolation. Satan hopes that at this point, that isolation will include a separation from God and all support mechanisms. This also happens with addictions.

However, as difficult as all this sounds, there is help available. Professional psychologists and psychiatrists understand these components. Ministers and other theological professionals understand the spiritual side of healing and both can help those suffering to understand what it is that they are experiencing and provide them with the hope that they can be healed. There is also family counseling which helps the entire family understand what they face and how to find and give support, seek solutions, and obtain healing for those they love and for themselves as well. It can uncover hidden pain that one or more family members have concealed which can cause their own form of depression.

Seeking help, assistance, and support is the courageous and well-grounded choice to make. It breaks the chain of helplessness and demonstrates self-determination. It opens the channels of communication and provides an outlet for ones concerns while assuring family members that help is on its way. While many in one family may have varying responses to a similar concern, family counseling can provide for everyone. There may be one family member who has displaced their anger, harbors a grudge or blames themselves. This can exacerbate the problem causing it to spread to all family members and often causes a withdrawal of one or more family members making resolution more difficult. Few people agree to face conflict head on. Most of us want to avoid conflict.

Conflict in itself has many components. Its characteristics are based in contradictory goals.

Counselors try to determine what form of conflict families might engage in so they can re-direct the conflict toward a resolution. One form of conflict is termed the "Approach-Approach Conflict" which requires choosing from two positive alternatives and is the easiest conflict to resolve. "Avoidance-Avoidance Conflict" which is based on choosing between two negative alternatives is characterized by vacillation. Finally, there is the "Approach-Avoidance Conflict" which is the most complex and produces the most ambivalence.

Conflict can cause both real and imagined ("psychosomatic") illnesses because of the high level of unpredictable stress involved. Either type of illness can cause real physical and even psychological damage. Again, this is reason for consulting professionals and obtaining their help to sort out the conflicts and determine how to solve them. Additionally, they may discover that there are others in the family who suffer silently and may also require help.

What might have caused the depression is also important. The death of a spouse for instance is rated as the number one stressor and a contributor to illness. A divorce, a marital separation, the death of a family member, the loss of a job, or the loss of one's health are also rated very high as stressors.

One reaction to depression is denial which is one of the most primitive and easily accessible protective mechanisms available. By ignoring our problem we can pretend that it does not exist and that we need not put forth the effort required to fix it. Denial temporarily protects us from experiences we fear may overwhelm us but it can prolong the problem.

Sometimes termed "psychological closure", denial can help our mind adjust to what may be extremely difficult to accept. Thus it can be used by the body as a defense mechanism. However, long term denial is dangerous and can lead to other psychological conditions such as repression, suppression, regression, reaction formation or fantasy, or even aggression and other conditions which may temporarily help one cope. Other reactions may be isolation, withdrawal, intellectualization, rationalization, compensation, and sublimation.

Again, these tell us that it requires a professional to help us sort out the many psychological reactions we have exhibited toward our concerns. A professional can also help us learn the art of introspection so we can understand where in ourselves the help and change is required. The examining of oneself, both past and present is of utmost importance to one's immediate and long-term healing. However, it takes a conscientious, well trained, concerned professional to engage their patients in this manner.

As mentioned in the beginning of this chapter, there may be a biochemical component to how one responds to their emotions or thoughts. It is believed that our neurotransmitters affect our mood and that a shortage of these produces depression. Again there are two approaches for addressing this healing component. One is through the use of a patented chemical medication such as an anti-depressant drug. Another is through a combination of nutritional therapies.

Some physicians believe that a deficiency in neurotransmitters is the cause of depression and that an increase in our natural essential amino acids can eliminate depression. Others believe that a combination of anti-depressant drugs and an individualized combination of essential amino acids along with other nutritional therapies will allow the tapering off of the drugs and thereby reduce the side effects which might occur through their use.

According to a newsletter written by Dr. Jonathan V. Wright titled *Nutrition & Healing*, Volume 18, Issue 8, October 2011, there are basically three major categories of patented chemical anti-depressants. These are Mono-amine oxidase inhibitors (MAOI's), Tricyclics, and Serotonin re-uptake inhibitors (SSRI's). These have a long list of side effects and must be taken continuously to artificially increase the number of neurotransmitter molecules in the synapses between neurons and prolong their activity. Most psychiatrists recommend one of these medications for pronounced depression.

However, and according to Dr. Wright, nutritional therapy claims that if the body could create more neurotransmitters, depression could be prevented or relieved. Studies show that neurotransmitters are produced from the essential amino acids which human's cannot create and must thereby come from the foods we eat. This approach warns that it is important to create the proper balance of all of the essential amino acids rather than succumb to the claims of any one or two amino acids found on the shelves of the health food stores which tout a healing. Again seeking professional help is important and proper nutritional therapy may offer an alternative to chemical anti-depressants.

Science does not yet know enough about the incredible complexities of brain biochemistry. However, science has determined various methods with which to combat some of the problems which arise from deficiencies and that we do not have the enzymes required for the biosynthesis of the essential amino acids. Dr. Wright states that a "fasting plasma essential amino acid" test can determine amino acid deficiencies to indicate what amino acids need to be augmented if one is utilizing the nutritional approach.

Blood tests can determine and manage the levels of the patented chemical medications which are prescribed to assure their effectiveness and minimize their side effects. Personalized and professional treatment assures the overall health of the patient and can determine whether low amino acids are a result of poor digestion or assimilation, or poor assimilation due to undetected non-celiac gluten sensitivity which may require additional treatment.

It may seem daunting to identify the various terms and protocols related to finding relief from depression, but to do so will provide an awareness of why we may be suffering. It teaches us how to participate in the healing process and to understand that it is a condition which can be reversed and this gives us hope.

NOTES

Photography by Colette van Loggerenberg

Pietermaritzburg, South Africa

Chapter Eleven

PEACE AND SELF-ESTEEM

Those who see the silver lining in every circumstance and find their cup half full rather than half empty are those who seem to rise effortlessly above even the most difficult circumstances. If such an attitude were for sale, we would purchase as much as we could afford! Since all of us face problems which make our lives difficult, it is natural to wonder how others seem to bear their circumstances with little concern. What makes one person happy and another saddened by similar events? Why is it that some become discouraged, frightened, impatient and heartbroken when life throws us a curve and others take it in stride? Why do some fall into depression and others do not? And how can we become more like those who bear their burdens with nobility?

Once again the answer lies in understanding our Adam-like nature and why scripture tells us to shed that nature and develop a Christ-like nature. God provides us with everything we could possible want, or need, out of His incredible love for us, but we do not always understand how to use what is offered. Our Heavenly Father often guides us to those who can help us whether this is a minister, a friend or a physician. Through prayer we can be assured that wherever our steps take us, if they are guided by our Heavenly Father, they will be blessed and will work to our benefit. The best thing that we can do for ourselves is first seek the kingdom of heaven…and then all will be added to us. God's guidance is not just found in our prayers, our tithes, our attending church, or our fellowship with other believers, but reaches out into all aspects of our life and brings us what we need.

Understanding scripture helps us acknowledge that every resource found in the world has been provided by our Heavenly Father and developed for our use. But we also have to understand the role which Satan plays and how he uses our human nature to bring us harm. Part of this is learning about the Adam-like nature which came into being when Adam and Eve sinned, brought the knowledge of both good and evil into our lives and forced development of the need to defend and sustain ourselves along with the emotions required to alert us to these needs.

Sin by disobedience separated Adam and Eve from God and took from them His perfect care. Thus, to survive *without* the all encompassing conversation, protection and provision they'd had from God, Adam and Eve's nature developed the automatic responses within their nervous system and stored memories in the temporal lobe of their brain which were, for the first time, negative. This phenomenon assured the continuation of the species through an automatic response. Mankind fell into what psychology terms “conditioning” as a protection and a drive which would assure their safety and sustenance. This occurred because of sin and produced the negativity with which we view our lives. Guilt, depression, hopelessness, and anger create the conclusion that God does not hear our pleas and that we are unworthy of God’s intervention.

Because we all sin, Satan has a huge platform from which to accuse us of how little we deserve from God. Further, what Satan whispers to us is true! We don’t deserve God’s help. Nevertheless, God does help us because He and the Lord Jesus see our potential and hope to make of us a worthy bride! Thus God has provided us with an understanding of our human nature and the drives it commands. He shows us how to move into a Christ-like nature of trust so we can avoid the traps Satan lays for us through the Adam-like nature.

Our Heavenly Father is omnipresent…. meaning that He is continuously and simultaneously present throughout the whole of creation. He is also omnipotent…. meaning that He possesses complete, unlimited, universal power and authority. Thus, we know that He can change our circumstances if He chooses to do so and often uses the natural components of our universe (which He created for this purpose) to do so. From this we learn that it is not a matter of whether or not we CAN be helped but a matter of us believing that God WILL help. If we break this down into the impact this has on the process through which we deal with heartache, we must first understand the Adam-like nature and why we must overcome it. This however, does not negate the fact that sometimes we need to reach out to our physicians and ministers, our mentors, and perhaps other professionals for the help God provides through them.

Scripture teaches us that God can bless those to whom we turn if we have asked for His protection and guidance. He will provide godly wisdom to those to whom He sends us because He loves us and cares for us. God's love is unconditional and eternal because it is love in its purest form while we think of love in earthly terms where it can be fickle and may have diminished our ability to trust. Satan wants us to become conditioned to experiencing disappointment, fear, distrust and selfishness and thus unable to fully trust God. Satan can prevent us from seeking help if we do not trust that God reaches all people and all places and all things as He sees fit to provide us with help. It is not always through a miracle that we are helped.

Let us imagine for a moment that we are young children attending pre-school. The teacher is God and the bully in the classroom is Satan. The teacher wisely allows the bully to act so the students can learn what comes of being a bully. The teacher seeks to help the students choose goodness over cruelty, develop empathy for those who are bullied, and learn how to stand up to and ultimately overcome a bully's tactics. The students initially react with fear when the bully attacks, but over time learn that the teacher protects them before harm can befall them and they begin to trust the teacher's intervention. Thus those who develop confidence in the teacher believe they will be protected. They know the teacher, have noted the teacher's past actions, and trust that past deeds predict future deeds and thus will protect them. But those who do not know the teacher or the constancy of that teacher's deeds have not developed the confidence required to feel protected when accosted by the bully. ***They haven't paid attention*** and continue to react with fear while the students who were at first "conditioned" to fear the bully (The Adam-like nature) have now been "conditioned" to trust the teacher (The Christ-like nature).

Early in the twentieth century, a Russian scientist named Ivan Pavlov gained international recognition through an experiment he conducted with a dog. Food was offered to the dog immediately after the ringing of a bell, and in time the dog salivated whenever he heard a bell ring whether or not food was provided. This demonstrated the impact of memory on automatic reactions to current situations.

A year earlier an American graduate student named E. B. Twitmeyer accidently conditioned the patella reflex (knee jerk) of a human subject to the ringing of a bell. Because people do not always meet our expectations, our Adam-like nature is conditioned to expect the worst when something unpleasant occurs. We become fearful and lose the self-esteem which provides us with our sense of self-empowerment. We fear what has occurred and become anxious, depressed and sometimes hopeless. Thus, examining what creates a happy person, despite a bevy of concerns, shows us that it is an attitude; a "conditioning" which prevents us from believing that help is on the way or that a change will be beneficial.

Unhappiness is actually a lack of trust in God's plan for us. It is a conditioning to expect the worst and not to expect a blessing. But **God has always been, is, and always will be trustworthy**.

His love is pure and perfect and never fails. When we are faithful and ask for His help, He is at our side. Thus when we internalize this phenomenon we become "conditioned" in belief, faith and trust and can overcome our concerns. **Fear is thwarted by faith**. We can lose our faith when we allow Satan to make us feel unworthy by reminding us that we are sinners and thus unworthy of happiness or of God's help. This negates the sacrifice of Christ and the gift of the forgiveness of sin….again, exactly what Satan wants us "conditioned" to believe.

When fear appears, if we routinely list the times past when God protected us and actively tell ourselves that we have no need to worry, we can re-condition our memories. We must remind ourselves of God's love and that with the forgiveness of sin **God no longer remembers our sin and places our striving above our failures**. God understands what our Adam-like nature does to us and speaks to us through scripture telling us not to fear. Hebrews 13:5 says that He will never leave us or forsake us and in Isaiah 43:2 that He will be with us. Exodus 33:22 tells us that God will cover us with His hand, Jeremiah 33:3 promises that if we call, He will answer, and John 14:27 tells us not to let out heart be troubled. We must repeat these words to ourselves every day until we know them so well that they become a part of our internal belief system. As we practice these words and begin to trust in them…thus trust God… in time inordinate concern will leave and no matter what befalls us, *if we are striving*, we will believe that God will see us through all our concerns and create a blessing from them. **We will become conditioned to react with our Christ-like nature which finds peace through trust in the Father.**

When Daniel walked into the lion's den, and Shadrach, Meshach and Abednego walked into the fiery furnace, they believed that God would look after them because they **chose** to believe this. Free will is not just the choice to do good or evil, to bring harm or love, or to eat a second piece of cake or not, but it is also to **choose how to think and**

what to believe. 1 Thessalonians 5:17 tells us to pray incessantly which is another way to condition our thinking and strengthen our faith! Being happy is employing the art of trust. It is ours for the asking and then the taking. **God wants us to be happy and offers us the means by which we can be happy.** Trusting Him with everything in our life creates in us the child who comes to the Father knowing that the Father will care for them. We may not break our fear overnight, but in time by listening to our own words repeating God's words which tell us that we need not fear, we will overcome.

A compelling alternative to unhappiness is to truly trust in God's plan for us and thank Him for His help. Scripture encourages us to trust God and through that trust find the peace God wants for us. 1 Corinthians 14:33 says, *"For God is not the author of confusion, but of peace....."* Galatians 5:22 tells us, *"But the fruits of the Spirit is love, joy, peace....."* And Colossians 3:15 says, *".....and let the peace of God rule in your hearts."* Further, scripture tells us not to lose our peace if we enter a home that is not worthy of our testimony. This verse further supports our need for fellowship with other believers to strengthen us.

Matthew 10:13 warns, *"And if the house be worthy, let your peace come upon it: but if it not be worthy, let your peace return to you."* Luke 18:1 tells us, *"And he spake a parable unto them to this end, that men ought always to pray, and not to faint."* As we move into the end times, God tells us to gather steadfastly in fellowship and the breaking of bread (Acts 2:42), and to bear one another's burdens (Galatians 6:2) and to pray without ceasing (1 Thessalonians 5:17). Through these activities we will be strengthened in faith and better equipped to retain our peace. Scripture also tells us that to know and acknowledge God is *"health to thy navel, and marrow to thy bones."* (Proverbs 3:8) This suggests that when we learn God's words, do as He asks, and seek a close relationship with Him, that the peace which we gain will keep our bodies, mind and spirit strong. Perhaps we can avoid the damage we do to ourselves from our fears and our stress and thus avoid many of the illnesses resulting from our emotions.

Similarly, a lack of self-esteem, which grows out of a lack of understanding, can harm every aspect of our lives. It creates fear and anxiety and adversely affects our relationships, including our relationship with God. This too can affect our health and well being. Without self esteem, without a sense of who we are and what we stand for, we cannot be spiritually successful spouses, parents, friends, neighbors or co-workers for we cannot be effective children of God. The loss of self-esteem can also make us fearful about what others may think of us and cause us to misinterpret a word or action. We may find something to be negative which was not meant to be negative.... Again, and unnecessarily, increasing our level of stress.

Proverbs 3:3-6 tells us, "*Let not mercy and truth forsake thee; bind them about thy neck; write them upon the table of thine heart. So shalt thou find favor and good understanding in the sight of God and man. Trust in the Lord with all thine heart; and lean not to your own understanding. In all thy ways, acknowledge him and he shall direct thy paths."*

These words are incredibly beautiful and assure us that if we hold to God's truth, whatever we do, wherever we go, whatever betides us, God will direct our path and keep us safe. It tells us that we should not trust in our own understanding of a situation but rather trust God with all our heart. We can be comforted by reading these many promises which scripture teaches us and which are given to us directly from God. We are also comforted by yet another scripture which teaches us that God wants us to find peace. Christ Himself speaks to us in John 14:27 and says, *"Peace I leave with you, my peace I give unto you: not as the world giveth, give I unto you. Let not your heart be troubled, neither let it be afraid."* This tells us that as we pray we can ask that Christ give us the peace He promises us, and ask that it may be added to whatever little peace we already have and thereby we will never be afraid.

Thus trusting God implicitly helps us remain healthy, physically, mentally and spiritually and by simply employing a few activities on our part we can have all that He promises. The following six actions are what scripture tells us will give us all that we need:

1. Learn what God wants us to know and do our best to follow His admonitions.

2. Have fellowship with other true believers who understand the virtues of love, compassion and trust.

3. Pray unceasingly, thanking God for every circumstances and what He will bring from them.

4. Condition our thinking to know that God will help us and loves us. Memorize some of the scripture which describes God's loving protection.

5. Be willing to seek professional help where and when needed and trust in it. Pray and offer and meet with our bearer of blessing so that where we go and the advice we seek will have the blessing from on High which we seek.

6. Ask for the peace which both God and Christ promised and ask that it carry us into the First Resurrection.

When we have done these things and then trust our Heavenly Father, He will always see us through. Understanding that God uses all the resources He has placed into this world as a way to bless us will help us move outside our comfort zone. There are many verses from scripture which can inspire us in times of need. Locating those verses which we love the best, writing them down, memorizing them and repeating them to ourselves many times during the day will help us know that God is always at our side.

Depression takes many forms and can arise from a loss, fear, frustration or chemical imbalance. Identifying the psychological aspects includes an assessment of whether the depression arises from an internal, external or personal source, whether or not it can be changed or is out of one's control, and whether or not one's persistence will be rewarding or futile. This helps distinguish between a real obstacle and an imagined obstacle and thus determine how the depression can best be treated. Identifying a chemical imbalance is also important so that a specific diet or specific medication may be determined necessary to healing. That said, we must understand that scripture also plays an important part in the healing process. A relationship with God provides hope, builds trust, offers a healing of the soul but also directs us to those who can help us. God has the power to guide us to whomever He wishes. If we ask in prayer that our Heavenly Father help us recognize what we need, provide those who will help us, provide wisdom to those who help us, and give power to what we ingest, we can be assured of His perfect help. Knowing what scripture tells us and learning about our psychological or physical condition allows us to participate in our healing process and also allows others to learn how they can provide support.

But the bottom line is learning what God wants us to know. Understanding the immensity of what He offers us, not only for our future as the Bride of Christ, but also here on earth so we may, despite what Satan may do, can live in peace and joy.

Nothing will work as well as first seeking and obtaining the blessing of our Heavenly Father, of learning to love Him and trust Him. With this in place, all ills, all crosses, all trials and tribulations can be lightened and borne more easily. All troubles can become a blessing and our future will be assured.

NOTES

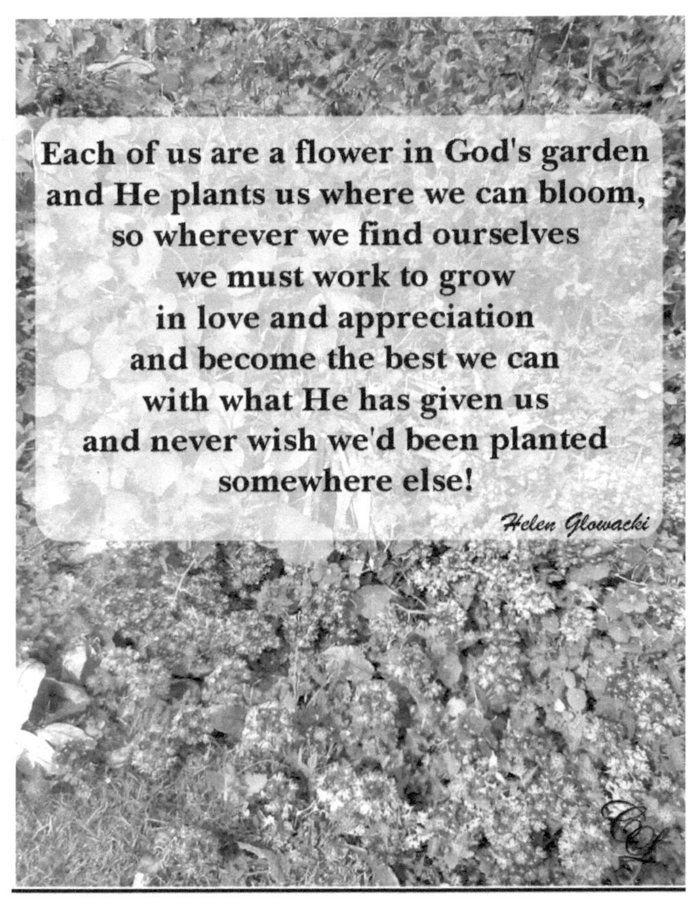

Photography by Colette van Loggerenberg

Pietermaritzburg, South Africa

Chapter Twelve

TO HEAL OR NOT TO HEAL

Sometimes we have to decide whether or not we have become comfortable where we are and really have no desire to change….or whether or not we want to be healed. Psychologically we can "get stuck" where we are and not realize that we are blocking our own progress emotionally, physically and spiritually.

Many of our reactions originate from how our parents reacted as do many of our fears and many of our traditions. Our parents' personality, which psychologists often call the “unique and enduring behavior pattern” is a combination of attitude, talent and habits. Their character describes how they behave and the value they place on honor and integrity. Their temperament describes their mood or emotional nature. As children we witness these traits of those close to us day in and day out and often adopt many of them ourselves.

But then comes a time when we must step back from the influence our parents had on us and look objectively at how they lived their lives. We must evaluate what effect their lives had on us, and if it is what we want for our own lives and the lives of our children. Sometimes we continue to agree with what our parents taught us and we follow their example, sometimes we keep some examples and create new ones, and in some cases, we may reject what our parents did… and even reject what they thought and believed. This is the process of becoming an adult and the process of learning right from wrong. As adults we must decide which path we want our lives to take and what kind of a role model we wish to become. We may often make adjustments as we grow wiser or we may decide to embark on a totally new path. We may make changes in our spiritual lives as we learn God's words. Marriage, children, heartache, someone we admire and respect can be the impetus for change and can be a force for good or, conversely, a force which draws us into complacency about God's words.

But as we mature, hopefully we begin to realize that how we act and which values we choose to espouse will affect our children and our future. We also realize that we will not only be held accountable for our own soul salvation but also for our children's soul salvation. Scripture clearly tells us that we are responsible for teaching our children God's words and that if we fail to do this we will be held accountable. We can also learn how to be a good parent from scripture and how to bring God's blessing to our homes and family.

Scripture is amazing in that all the psychological components discussed in earlier chapters can be understood through God's words in scripture. We can learn how to treat one another, how to pray, how to ask God for healing, why we are subject to spiritual invasion and evil and how this can cause our various illness, addictions, and tendencies. We are taught about God's plan of salvation and why we must struggle to grow closer to God. We learn about Satan and the role he plays in our lives, and we learn about death and life after death.

We also learn about the Adam-like nature with which we are born and which offers all the components which the field of psychology addresses. We learn why we need to overcome that nature and leave it behind so that we can grow into the Christ-like nature which God will require of us to become the bride of Christ. We learn about success and failure and the forgiveness we can obtain despite our failures. We learn how to be an overcomer and how to thwart the evil which Satan wants to bring us.

What we learn from scripture can change us; transform us from the shallow life of material possessions to the gifts of a spiritual life which has far greater reward. We learn that God can turn our heartache into a blessing for us. We learn that as our trust in our Heavenly Father increases our fear diminishes, and we learn how to be content.

We learn that time as we know it was not put into place until the end of the fourth day of the creation which Genesis describes as the moment when the sun and moon were put into place and time as we know it began. Thus the carbon dating of evolution is compatible with scripture and the scientists wrong in telling us that this refutes the value of scripture. We learn that scripture describes the end times and what we must do to prepare for it. And we learn what our most difficult test will be.

Scripture also teaches us about choosing those who will govern us and how to test doctrine through the fruits of the Holy Spirit. We learn how sin came into this world and why and what will happen to all sinful things after Judgment day. Thus we learn of the Lake of Fire and what the second death means. We learn who Christ will take for the First Resurrection and what will happen to Satan and those who scripture calls the "goats".

We learn that the Apostles of Christ went out to extend God's offer of salvation to everyone who ever lived or died. We learn that they could heal and cast out the spirits which brought illness and addiction and heartache, or compounded generational sin.

But most of all we learn about love. Real love… pure love…not the kind of self-serving love we first thought so important. We learn how much God loves us and we learn to trust Him with everything in our life. We learn that His love is so great that

He forgives our sin. We learn what it means to take Holy Communion worthily and what that requires of us. We learn that God can see into our heart and **loves the heart which strives to please Him** despite the failures Satan might bring.

We know that healing physically and mentally can occur even in those who do not seek God and even in those who spurn God. But real healing occurs when the soul is healed and the body follows with its healing of the relationship we seek with God. We learn that the healing of our soul brings us the ability to bloom where we are planted and to become a blessing to others. And we learn that the healing of our soul brings us peace and allows us to combine faith and works to please God and bring us a blessing.

We learn that God can place into our lives the people who can help us and the paths we are to take to bring us to a better life.

When our soul has been freed of the sin Satan brings we can truly, truly appreciate, truly trust and truly grow into the beautiful and perfect Bride which our Heavenly Father seeks for His Son. We never have to fear the Lake of Fire or Judgment Day, but can rest assured that we will be a part of the Bride and thus a part of the First Resurrection.

NOTES

"And God

shall wipe away

all tears from their eyes;

and there shall be

no more death,

neither sorrow, nor crying,

neither shall there be

any more pain. . . ."

Revelation 21:4

ABOUT THE AUTHOR

Helen Glowacki is an interior designer, writer, teacher, and motivational speaker. As the host, writer, and producer of the television series "The Contemporary Woman", broadcast by UA Columbia Cablevision, she addressed interior design and the health, relationship, parenting, and life issues of interest to women. She has co-hosted a number of 24-hour telethons featuring celebrity guests, and was a guest co-host for a cable television game show. Her writing credentials include an extensive background as a freelance feature writer and a staff writer for four newspapers, newsletters, marketing manuals, and the designer and editor of two association newsletters.

A graduate of William Paterson University, Helen received her Bachelor of Arts degree in Communications, magna cum laude. She also earned an Associate of Science degree, with honors, and is a registered nurse. She has served on the

Boards of Directors for two associations and taught interior design for adult school programs.

Helen was listed in *Who's Who of American Women* and *Who's Who of Women Executives,* is a popular speaker at ease with an audience and addresses aspects of interior design, specifically through the application of Divine Proportion, and the work of God and His word through Scripture. Helen also uses the poems she has written, which appear intermittently in her books, to describe God's help in times of difficulty. Her venues have included women's groups, church groups, community service and religious organizations, high schools and colleges, in libraries, on cruise ships, and in large adult and assisted living condominium complexes and as a guest on a radio show, and in theater groups, army camps, and veteran's hospitals.

Profits from the sale of her books go into providing them to various cancer centers, drug rehabilitation centers, and prisons, and to the mission schools of

The Henwood Foundation in Zambia, Africa. Those who have provided reviews of Helen's books tout her beautiful stories as spiritually uplifting and biblically correct.

Helen's greatest joys are her husband, two children, four grandchildren, and her time spent in her New Apostolic Church and in fellowship. Her heart's desire is to help others find the love and comforting presence of God through her writing, her interaction with others, her love of research, her remarkable knowledge and interpretation of scripture, and her multiple outreach activities. She has written for Christian magazines and newsletters, Bible study groups, and various other applications. Her joy in teaching others of God's magnificent gifts inspires and strengthens her to work every day to touch as many hearts as possible.

For additional copies of this book visit
www.helenglowacki.com

Photography by Colette van Loggerenberg

Pietermaritzburg, South Africa

BIBLIOGRAPHY

New Apostolic Church. *The Holy Bible* (King James Version). Canada: Thomas Nelson, Inc., 1972.

New Apostolic Church. *The Holy Bible* (New King James Version). North America: Thomas Nelson Publishers, 1994.

Strong, James. *Strong's Exhaustive Concordance of the Bible.* Abington, Nashville, 1890.

New Revised Standard Version of the Apocrypha, Oxford University Press, Inc., 1991

Dr. Jonathan V. Wright's *Nutrition & Healing* Newsletter, Volume 18, Issue 8, October 2011

Photography by David Campbell
Boca Raton, Florida United States

Excerpt from:

WHAT NO ONE TELLS YOU ABOUT ADDICTION

Written in an easy to read and easy to understand manner, this is one of the most interesting books ever written about addictions. From alcohol and drug addictions to homosexuality, pedophilia and kleptomania, the lusts of these satanic captivities are finally explained through scripture.

Few understand spiritual warfare and the spirits which can enter mankind and cause a hunger for that which is displeasing to God. The power of these hungers can be overwhelming and produce such a strong need to feed the invading spirit that those who are captive are often driven to a life of crime and sometimes to their own death. Recognizing what inspires these satanic invasions, what allows them to stay, and what they require to exist, provides a great incentive to seek one's freedom from the slavery they impose. Scripture aptly and clearly describes what is required to create the environment which causes these spirits to leave the soul which they have invaded.

This book also provides some helpful facts about recognizing and overcoming the selfish co-dependency of the enabler and how they mistakenly believe that they are helping the addict when in fact they are encouraging the addict to remain under the captivity of their addiction. "Tough love" and what scripture explains about sin, and a description of generational sin and the tendencies mankind may inherit, and must fight, provides an explanation of why families often find father and son or mother and daughter falling into similar patterns.

This non-fiction book will help those seeking to understand the strength of an addiction and the personality changes which often accompany addiction. It will help the reader understand why God allows this heartache and what can be done to break its hold on those we love and wish to help by also providing the supporting scripture which describes spiritual invasion. Applying scripture to real life situations helps the reader learn about God's plan of Salvation and about the enemy who has waged war with God.

Helen's books also address the forgiveness of sin and why God will accept a repentant sinner as a part of the Bride of Christ and what to expect after death.

This book, like all the books written by this author is a must read!

Photography by Matthew Burniston

City of Bradford, West Yorkshire, England

List and Description of Novels

by Helen Glowacki (Book Size 6 x 9)

When God Broke Grandma's Heart: (208 pages) Rising from sorrow to become a beacon of faith Grandma struggles in an abusive marriage until God moves her from unequally yoked and broken to the healing of His love and forgiveness. Her granddaughter Sarah learns where to find answers to her problems and carries that legacy to those she loves. **Paperback: ISBN 978-0-9847-2110-8**

When God Took Grandma Home: (260 pages) About the heartache of drug addiction, of the enemy who destroys children through drugs, why God allows righteous anger, why we should pray for those in eternity and a description an incredible experience of faith for Matt and Sarah about why God allowed such heartache to occur.

Paperback: ISBN 978-0-49847-2111-5

When Grandma Chased the Spirits: (208 Pages) The magnetism of idolatry, it's invisible power, and the heartache of bearing a child out of wedlock brings debilitating panic attacks to Mary and affects her husband Kevin. When Matt and Sarah tell them about their faith, God engineers a miracle to solve what that they thought impossible to resolve. **Paperback: ISBN 978-0-9847-2112-2**

The Granddaughter and the Monkey Swing: (284 pages) A wedding, a broken engagement, renovating and decorating a home through Divine Proportion, the truth about Halloween, and the gift of role models create a tender story of friendship. Helping through the planning and problems of a wedding culminates in the unveiling of a secret. **Paperback: ISBN 978-0- 9847-2113-9**

Grandma's Little Book of Poetry: The Story of God's Plan of Salvation: (277 pages) This beautiful whimsical story for all ages, begins when Sarah finds a manuscript in Grandma's desk and recognizes the story Grandma read to her and Josh and Caleb when they were children. Angels watch the inhabitants below them struggle to find God.

Paperback: ISBN 978-0-9847-2114-6

Abiding Faith, Hidden Treasure: (262 pages) Serving in Iraq, Jim loses his faith to see a loving God allow so much heartache. Barbara invites him to dinner where Grandma shows him why creation and evolution co-exist and God's enemy creates the injustices Jim blames on God. Letters from the grave bring an incredible experience of faith.

Paperback: ISBN 978-0-9847-2115-3

And Then They Asked God: (295 Pages) When Rebecca and Jayden arrive at their college campus they are overwhelmed by betrayal. Losing the values Rebecca once cherished fills her with guilt so monumental that she cannot forgive herself. Chaldeth the evil angel is defeated when God's grace frees Jayden and brings Rebecca's recovery.

Paperback: ISBN 978-0-9847-2116-7

List of the "Why God Why" mini-series by Helen Glowacki

(Book Size 5 ½ x 8)

To What Purpose?: (126 pages) This first book in the *Why God Why* series answers questions about why we are here, what we need to learn, and what God plans for us. It is an excellent book for testimony and one you will share with others.

Paperback: ISBN 978-1-4507-7580-9

Why God, Why?: (126 pages) This second book in the *Why God Why* Series describes why we experience heartache, its purpose, and how to face it. It answers questions about God's plan for us and what we need to do to be found worthy.

Paperback: ISBN 978-1-4507-7581-6

Why Trust Scripture?: (126 pages) This third book in the *Why God, Why* Series addresses the challenges against scripture, who wrote the Bible, the importance of the sacraments, what role Satan plays, and how health and the Bible are related.

Paperback: ISBN 978-1-4507-7582-3

What Should I Know about Life after Death and the Coming Tribulation?: (126 pages) What occurs following death, what will happen during the tribulation, and what the seven seals could mean to us are explained in this fourth book of the series.

Paperback: ISBN 978-1-4507-7583-0

What Does God Want Me to do Right Now?: (126 pages) A concise explanation of what God asks of us, how we can live up to His expectations what is required to become a part of the Bride of Christ, and what God plans for the future with or without us.

Paperback: ISBN 978-1 4507-9076-5

Coming Soon

Do The Little Sins Really Count? (126 pages) Most of us believe that the little sins don't really matter but scripture explains why they do.

List of Non-Fiction Books
By Helen Glowacki

(Book Size 5 ½ x 8 ½)

Politically Incorrect: The Get Some Gumption Bible Study When Enough is Enough: (298 pages) Fifty timely and controversial issues are examined under the politically correct approach along with a description of what scripture says is the approach that He wants his children to take.

Paperback: ISBN 978-1-4507-9074-1

The Many Faces of Depression: How Can I Be Happy?: (258 pages) We all face heartache, and all feel sad from time to time. But depression lingers and can result from many different causes. It can rob us of hope and destroy our relationship with God. Thus our Heavenly Father tells us through scripture how we can tap into His blessing and His direction and brings joy out of tribulation.

Paperback: ISBN 978-1-4507-9077-2

<u>What No One Tells You About Addictions</u>: (216 pages) Discussing the merits of tough love, the selfish co-dependency of the enabler, what scripture tells us about spiritual warfare and invasion, and generational sin, make this book a must read.

Paperback: ISBN 978-1- 4507--9075-8

Book Reviews

Reverend (District Apostle Ret.) Richard C. Freund, President of The New Apostolic Church, USA, Sea Cliff, New York: Magnificent writer, a story which makes the reader become emotionally involved, a joy to read, strong Christian values. ***"When God Broke Grandma's Heart",*** best seller quality.

Reverend (District Apostle Ret.) Richard C. Freund, President of The New Apostolic Church, USA. Helen's new novel, ***"When God Took Grandma Home"*** "Delights, brings comfort to those who grieve. Inspires, gives insight into the after-life, masterful portrayal.

Reverend Andrew Muliokela: New Apostolic Church in Alexandria, Virginia, formerly from Zambia Africa: ***The Granddaughter and the Monkey Swing*** and this series of books are awesome! A journey unlike another, I was reading a great novel, learning about confidence, love and support but also learning Bible verses at the same time! Helen Glowacki teaches through her books and I recommend them 100%. You'll enjoy the journey!

Reverend Frederick Rothe, (Ret. New Apostolic Church, New York) Palm Beach Gardens Congregation, Florida: Spent 48 years serving

God and another 30 in the congregation. These books contain an accurate account of what God wants of us and why we suffer. The application of scripture and the people in the stories stand for the principles God wants in all of us.

Reverend Kevin Speranza, New Apostolic Church, Palm Beach Gardens, Florida: ***And Then They Asked God*** so happy I read this, weaves, documents biblical precepts, addresses political correctness, moral & political corruption, biased teaching, insidious growth of socialism renamed progressivism, self-importance, guilt and its debilitating power. WELL DONE! Identifies danger, artfully and Biblically addresses them.

Reverend Luke Jansen, Sr. V. P., Medical Connections, Boca Raton, Florida: "To Ms. Glowacki, author of **The Grandma Series**: grateful for your books, refreshing to find a Christian author who sees the *difference* between religion and spirituality AND that the two can and should be used in the same sentence.

Reverend Derryck Beukes, Montana-De Aar Congregation, Northern Cape, South Africa: Dear Helen, I personally often use your articles in my soul care visits, especially where youth are involved. I can assure you that your articles made a difference to my way of thinking, and I am busy encouraging fellow priests to read your works, as they are so factual and insightful! Thank you for your hard work. I thank God for you, and the wisdom He gave you! Please continue with the excellent work.

Deacon Shadreck Wilima, Overspill Congregation, Ndola, Zambia: Your articles prompt realistic examples which New Apostolic Christians need for their everyday living.

Youth Chairperson, Sunday School Teacher, Mulenga Ernest, Lusaka Central Congregation, Lusaka, Zambia: Through your writing I am constantly reminded of what to be aware of. I pray that God keeps you in the hollow of His hand, guards you and guides you to reach your brethren as you do me. Thanks for caring for the souls of many.

Reverend Aurelio Cerullo, Atripalda Congregation in Campania, Southern Italy: Dear Helen, your books and articles, and social networking bring brothers and sisters the words of our faith and touch the hearts of those who do not know our faith. Our goal isfound through the grace of the apostolate and in this sense, the word's from 1 Corinthians 15:58 assumes an important meaning: "*Therefore, my beloved brethren, be steadfast, immovable, always abounding in the work of the Lord, Knowing That your labor is not in vain in the Lord*". Now that I am a minister of God for about a year I too am grateful to our beloved Father in Heaven for having opened the eyes of my soul, for having removed the plugs from my ears of my heart to hear and listen to His will in connection and communion with those who precede us, guided by the light of the Holy Spirit. God's work always evolves and adapts to the times and even via computers, cell phones and smart phones. I Thank God for having been able to know you, you're a very valuable pearl. God bless you richly.

Rev. Fred Krueger, (Ret.) Lutheran Minister 12 yrs and Clinical Social Worker 26 years, Dallas, Texas: "Inspiring, grabs the heart, author headed to the bestseller list, a pleasure to read, masterful. ***"When God Took Grandma Home"*** filled with insight into God's plan!

NOTE: The articles which are referred to in these reviews are excerpts from Helen Glowacki's non-fiction books. Not shown are reviews by the ministers who oversee *The Henwood Foundation*'s New Apostolic Mission Schools in Zambia and review all reading materials prior to distribution.

Edith Stier, wife of a Ret. District Evangelist, Clifton, New Jersey: *The Grandma Series* helps those in need, inspirational, heartwarming, ends with a beautiful example of how God explains our pain, renews hope, shows us the way, creates miracles. I love this series.

Patricia Robinson, wife of a Ret. Rector, Indiana
5 star rating: ***When God Broke Grandma's Heart***: WONDERFUL INSPIRATIONAL NOVEL, enjoyed this book, well written, Bible references, how to achieve peace of mind and soul .

Rosemarie Schaal, wife of an Ret. Reverend, New York: ***Abiding Faith, Hidden Treasure***: Reader develops empathy, feels emotion, hears a battle between scientific and spiritual knowledge. Skillful, detailed, brilliant, vivid, teaches nothing happens that is not planned by Him.

Colette van Loggerenberg, wife of a Minister, Scottsville Congregation of Pietermaritzberg, South Africa: *Grandma's Little Book of Poetry: The Story of God's Plan of Salvation:* This has to be one of the BEST EVER books that I have read....If you ever get the chance to get one of Helen's novels...READ IT. It's like a fairytale but a TRUE fairytale.....Close your eyes and picture this: Grandma with her hair in a bun, glasses perched delicately on her nose, sitting in a rocking chair and her grandchildren sitting on the floor with BIG eyes hanging onto her every word.....but with a twist!!!!! If you have doubts about PRAYER...read this book. I LOVED IT...thank you!

Debbie Espeland, wife of a Rector, Palm Beach Gardens Congregation, Florida: 5 star rating: ***When God Took Grandma Home***: HEARTWARMING! This book touched my heart. It is both heartwarming and very spiritual.

Aletta Venter, wife of a Deacon, Scottsville Congregation, Pietermaritzburg, South Africa: "*Grandma's Little Book of Poetry: The Story of God's Plan of Salvation*". What a learning process for me. Oooh I just **love** the way the angels are telling the story, **very original!** When is mankind ever going to learn? The inhabitant's lesson was to learn of good and evil. And they failed miserably each time. The devil has his agenda, and the inhabitants are the target. They call upon God for help, the angels rejoiced. Great….!!!

Aletta Venter, wife of a Deacon, Pietermaritzburg, South Africa: ***"Abiding Faith, Hidden Treasure"*** is the deepest and most rewarding novel I have ever read, touched my soul, made me cry, author's understanding of God's work is astounding, opens the mysteries

Lisa Mayo, wife of Minister, Palm Beach Gardens Congregation, Florida: Helen's ***Why God Why*** **series** of books gave me a new understanding of my faith. They are informative, so enlightening and in-depth, but in a way that is easily understood!!

Tammera Shelton, M.S. Psychology, Odenton, Maryland: I find ***"When God Broke Grandma's Heart"*** inspirational, beautifully portrays need to let go of negative events and that despite injustice, no pain is for naught.

Robert W. Rothe, USMC 1970-1976, Nevada: 5 star rating: ***When God Broke Grandma's Heart:*** Outstanding writer, kept me riveted, an angel sent to help through trying days. Thank you for helping me find peace.

Katharina Leipp, Schopfheim, Germany: This is the first time I have ever heard of a female New Apostolic author and I am very impressed by your articles. I have sent your link to my Shepherd and German friends and would like you to consider advertising in our German *Our Family Magazine.*

Claudine Visagie, South Africa: I'm trying to think of a way to introduce Helen's books and articles to others… especially to our youth. They are life changing!

Rabecca Mukuta Mukato, Lusaka, Zambia, Africa: Speaking on behalf of my Dad, District Elder Mukato, your articles are brilliant because they have changed me! Because of your articles my Dad has less headaches!

Robert Henry Parkes, Pietermaritzburg, South Africa: You are gifted with the verses and writings you do and are so inspiring to others. God is really using you as His special servant. You are really a wonderful person and we thank the Lord for you our sister in faith.

Frank Geores, from Port St. Lucie, Florida: "***When Grandma Chased The Spirits:*** beautiful spiritual experience, can see caring nature and loving heart of author, eloquently reveals her love for God and search for truth. Worthy of the Star of Bethlehem rating. Thank you for sharing your magnificent gift.

Ben Lodwick, Avid Reader., from Brookfield, Wisconsin: Wow! An eye opener about God's plan of salvation, and why bad things happen to good people. Reminds me of Jim LaHaye and Jerry B. Jenkins "Left Behind Series". MUST READ!"

Dr. Walter Forman From North Palm Beach, Florida: ***Grandma's Little Book of Poetry: The Story of God's Plan of Salvation:*** a "wonderful book about success and failure in life. All Helen's novels are wonderful, a balm for the soul and an education to the seeker."

Susan Day, From Jupiter, Florida: ***Abiding Faith, Hidden Treasure*** : I hated to put it down, couldn't wait to pick it up, read all Helen's books, proves every point, shows what to do through God's words. I am 90 and Helen's books have helped me call on God.

Georgette Rothe, From Fort Piece, Florida: ***Abiding Faith, Hidden Treasure*** was more than I expected; a Biblical course making you re-evaluate your beliefs, enjoyed the journey very much.

Fred D'Alauro, from Palm Beach Shores, Florida: Internet 5 star rating: ***When God Took***

Grandma Home: Remarkable! Inspirational, moving. Fascinating storyteller with a real message.

Debra Forman, Chester, New York. Internet 5 star rating: ***When God Broke Grandma's Heart**:* Written from the heart, shares the strong beliefs that shelters us in times of need, courage captivates the reader. Thank you.

Anonymous: Internet 5 star rating: ***When God Broke Grandma's Heart**:* WHEN LIFE GETS YOU DOWN, PICK THIS BOOK UP, it wrapped its arms around me. A wonderful read. Congratulations on an inspiring work.

A reviewer, a reader in Kentucky: Internet 5 star rating: ***When God Broke Grandma's Heart**:* Well written, heartwarming, overcoming heartbreak through God, touches your heart. A worthwhile read for all generations.

A reader: Internet 5 star rating: ***When God Broke Grandma's Heart:*** a must read for all generations. FANTASTIC!

A reviewer Internet 5 star rating: ***When God Took Grandma Home**:* Moves you, captivating.

A reviewer, a Kentucky reader: Internet 5 star rating: ***When God Took Grandma Home**:* MUST READ! Touching story of life's tragedies and how lessons learned from these heartbreaking events can turn into blessings.

Description of the Characters in the Novels By Helen Glowacki

Grandma: Grandma's life was filled with sibling betrayal and marital abuse. Her love of God, home remedies and famous boxing stance touches the heart.

Sarah: Sarah helps Grandma write her journal, learns about God's plan of salvation and the enemy who wants to harm her. She carries on Grandma's legacy of faith.

Matt: Matt, Sarah's husband, has a rock-like faith but when he loses a loved one, struggles with his anger with God, until he has a miraculous experience of faith.

Paul: Paul is Matt's older brother who earned a Captain's license for a seagoing tugboat. His faith sustains him despite enduring terrible circumstances.

Mary and Kevin: Mary and Kevin become Matt and Sarah's neighbors and friends. Mary's panic attacks end when God brings a miracle they never thought possible.

Elizabeth: Elizabeth adopts Rebecca, loses her husband twelve years later, is confronted with a potentially deadly illness and searches for Rebecca's birth mother.

Rebecca: Rebecca is Elizabeth daughter and Jayden's friend. Her father's death, the illness her mother faces, and a series of challenges at college almost destroy her.

John: John, a deacon, lost his wife to a debilitating disease, becomes Elizabeth's friend, and helps his daughter and grandson through a difficult divorce.

Jayden: Jayden is John's grandson and becomes Rebecca's friend. He has learned that prayer helps solve problems and he and Rebecca begin to share their faith.

Wade and Ruth: Wade is Jim's boss and friend who adopts two children from Iraq. Ruth is Jayden's mother and John's daughter who struggles to let go of the past.

Joshua and Debbie: Joshua, Sarah's younger brother, was demanding and judgmental until Caleb stepped in. Debbie looks to Joshua's family to be her role models.

Caleb and Ann: Caleb is Sarah and Josh's older brother and the family looks to him as they once looked to Grandma. Ann, Caleb's wife harbors a secret sadness.

Barbara and Jim: Barbara, Matt's sister is also Sarah's close friend. Her husband Jim plays devil's advocate in family debates, and matchmaker for his friend Wade.

Heza and Bara: Heza and Bara endured a suicide bomber attack when Bara was one and one half years old and Heza as she was born. They are adopted by Wade.

Chaldeth: Chaldeth is a fallen angel sent to destroy Grandma's family. He plots to bring great heartache to Rebecca and Jayden and their family to break their faith.

Durk: Durk, abused by a cruel father, is a sophomore at the college Rebecca and Jayden attend. He brings harm to Rebecca and Jayden but Jim gives him a second chance.

Professsor T. Nagorra, and Emils, and Dean Peerca:
These tenured professors befriend Durk and engage in activities that bring harm to the students and campus.

Professors Doog and Sendnik, and President Legna:
These three share a faith in God, a love for their country, and desire to be role models. They help save the campus.

"The Lord is my light

and my salvation;

whom shall I fear?

The Lord is the strength

of my life;

of whom

shall I be afraid?"

Psalm 27:1

www.ingramcontent.com/pod-product-compliance
Lightning Source LLC
LaVergne TN
LVHW090559110826
845146LV00001B/192

9781450790772